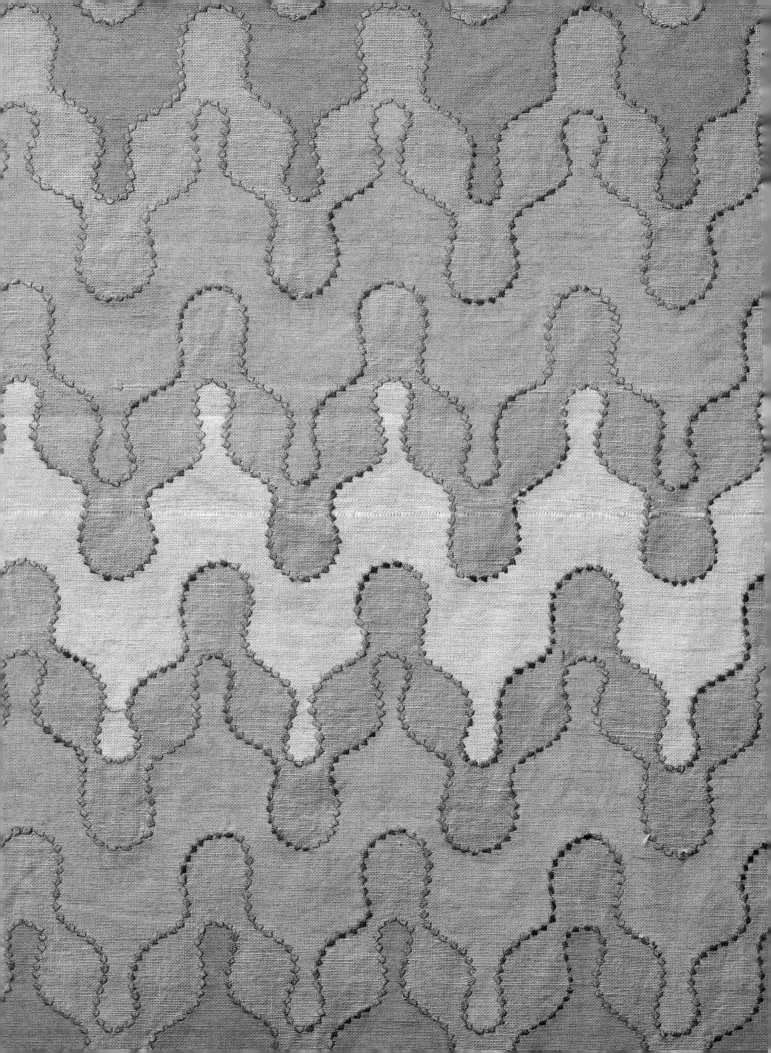

BARRY DIXON

INSPIRATIONS

BARRY DIXON INSPIRATIONS

Brian D. Coleman
Photographs by Erik Kvalsvik

GIBBS SMITH
TO ENRICH AND INSPIRE HUMANKIND

First Edition
15 14 13 12 11   5 4 3 2 1

Text © 2011 Brian D. Coleman
Photographs © 2011 Erik Kvalsvik, except as follows:
Pages 204–13, 218–21 © 2011 Gordon Beall
Pages 214–17 © 2011 Tria Giovan

Published by
Gibbs Smith
P.O. Box 667
Layton, Utah 84041

1.800.835.4993 orders
www.gibbs-smith.com

Designed by Debra McQuiston
Printed and bound in China

Gibbs Smith books are printed on either recycled, 100% post-consumer waste, FSC-certified papers or on paper produced from sustainable PEFC-certified forest/controlled wood source. Learn more at www.pefc.org.

Library of Congress Cataloging-in-Publication Data

Coleman, Brian D.
  Barry Dixon Inspirations / Brian D. Coleman ; Photographs by Erik Kvalsvik. — First Edition.
    pages cm
  ISBN 978-1-4236-0751-9
  1. Dixon, Barry (Barry Darr)—Themes, motives. 2. Interior decoration—United States. I. Title.
  NK2004.3.D58C653 2011
  747.092—dc22

                                                                          2010047799

Often the most profound inspiration comes from those around us, the ones we love and admire. Michael Schmidt has inspired me since the moment we met almost 20 years ago. Muses are all around us.

—B. D.

I thank my editor, Madge Baird, for helping us produce my fifteenth beautiful book and K. H. for his encouragement.

—B. C.

contents

Foreword

BY MICKEY RIAD, FORTUNY

Anyone can find inspiration in his or her surrounding environment. Though at times it may be difficult to find, inspiration is there, should one take the time to look. A common trait shared between true artists and designers is the ability to derive inspiration from what most people simply overlook or consider ordinary. Nevertheless, only a great artist is able to take that inspiration and create outstanding environments that not only exude a sense of balance and harmony but also inspire others through the simple act of existing in the same space. This, perhaps, may be Barry's greatest talent.

When Barry's name is mentioned in conversation, the first words that are often expressed typically include "charming," "gracious," "gentleman," and more often than not, all of the above. I have found that there are pretty much only two camps of people when it comes to Barry: those who love him and those who have not yet met him. In getting to know him these past couple of years, it is easy to see why. On their way to a meeting with my brother and me in New York not too long ago,

Barry and his associate, Laurel, were caught in a sudden rainstorm, which delayed them slightly. As apologetic as Barry was for being a few minutes late, he was more apologetic to Laurel for not having had the foresight to bring an umbrella with him from Warrenton, Virginia. "My mother always told me, 'You don't carry an umbrella for yourself. You carry it for the lady who is with you,'" Barry explained. A testament to the wonderful job his parents and family have done, Barry is so well mannered that he manages to bring out the best of those around him. No matter how many times we meet, it still strikes me just how utterly polite and pleasant he is, and how complete and undivided his attention is when engaged in conversation. He has this uncanny ability to make you feel as if you are the most important person in the world at that moment, and deserving of nothing less than the full respect and courtesy that he warmly extends.

This attitude is clearly reflected in Barry's work, as well. It is seen and, more importantly, felt in every room

he designs, where even the smallest of details is treated with deliberate consideration and care. Every detail has a story, and every story has its place in revealing the important part it plays in the overall artistic vision. The aesthetic beauty achieved through the thoughtful arrangement of objects and furnishings, each weighted with the history of its unique past, is infused with his endless passion and dedication, and lends an immeasurable and precious gravitas to the atmosphere of every environment he creates. As serious as his work may be, though, it comes across as effortless. Never afraid to drop a pun, it is obvious just how much fun Barry has doing what he does, as the laughs are just as much a part of the process as anything else.

In February of this year, my brother and I had the pleasure of spending a week in Ven-ice with Barry and Laurel for the installation of our newly renovated showroom. The plan was to begin installing on a Monday so that we could open the showroom on Friday. Yet, as is so very often the case with life, the plan and the reality of a situation can be two very different things, and in retrospect, I suspect that Murphy must have been conducting a live demonstration of his law in our showroom that week. Monday morning found us standing in a frigid construction zone, the beauty of our fabrics and the new floors virtually unrecog-nizable through the layers of dust and power tools, where before us columns were being in-stalled in the wrong place, the stairway was barely half built, the glass was cut to the wrong measurements and the only place the drop ceil-ing existed was on the drawing. And these were

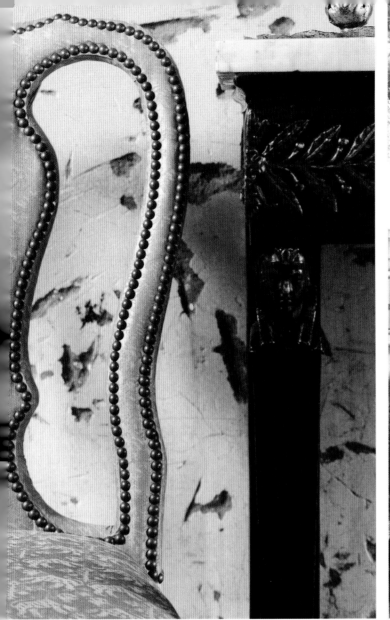

just the issues with the entryway. Throughout all the mishaps and surprises, though, Barry maintained a level of professionalism and grace that was truly inspirational and encouraging. While most people would have been enraged and lost their cool, Barry simply stated, "Well, that's not how I drew it," and then found a way to make it work. The eternal optimist, his perseverance never wavered for a moment, and he was right there with us on his hands and knees that Friday evening, scraping plaster and paint off the terrazzo so that we could slide the furniture into place a few minutes shy of midnight and open on schedule.

Through no small feat, Barry managed to make our fabrics appear even more beautiful. By fully embracing the magic and the illustrious history of our founder and craft and mas-

terfully marrying it to our vision and dreams, he provided the perfect platform from which we can tap deeper into our greatest source of pride and inspiration. In looking through the stunning images presented in this book, each more magnificent than the other, I am sure that every person who experiences these exquisite rooms cannot help but be inspired, as well, just as I am sure that Barry was equally inspired by the lives he created them for, their unique history and the distinctive qualities and charms particular to the soul he draws out of every individual place.

—Mickey Riad, *Vice President & Creative Director, Fortuny,* September 2010

Where Inspiration Lives

Inspiration is everywhere. It lives in the memory of our past, the vibrancy of our present and the possibility of our future. It hides in plain sight in the view outside our window and it sits on a shelf inside our home. It lurks in foreign ports of call and waits patiently in our own backyard. It whispers to us in our dreams and screams at us in our waking moments, urging that moment of glorious combustion when our thoughts collide to spark our imagination. From the hay fields outside my windows, to a trip to exotic Marrakesh, to a treasured cocoa tin from my childhood, the following trio explains three sources of my own inspiration. Look. Think. Create!

Crop Art Circles

The vivid clarity of a now long forgotten dream slowly succumbed to the hazy reality of another summer morning in Fauquier County. A steady drone of modern machinery had lured me from one state of consciousness to another, and I realized that the audio portion of my altered state was actually my friend Ricky cutting the tall grass in the pastures beyond the low stone walls that separate Elway Hall from Elway Farm. Peering through the windows of my bedroom aerie I could chart his progress: long furrowed rivulets of silken strands combed into place by the line of blades in his wake, such order in the concentric curves as he turned a graceful one-eighty to plod a parallel path in the vale.

Later he would roll the fallen straw into mammoth coils that would be left to dry further in the June sun. I always love the look of the rolling hills dotted with the large, sweet-smelling bales, their undulating forms crispened by the fresh, clean cut.

By July I noticed that he had, with deft efficiency, of course, stacked the rolled bales vertically two and three tall to keep them "high and dry." The resultant wall was like some wonderful, angle-less honeycomb—again with the mesmerizing op-art effect of the concentric circles at the bales' ends—that became a snapshot in my memory.

Ankasa

My Berber guide lured me farther and farther into the labyrinth of offerings that is Marrakesh's medina. Past tables of gigantic cones of exotic spices, past walls of pointy-toed and perky colored shoes that would have put a smile on Aladdin's face, past an arched opening that framed a beckoning array of antique lanterns of every size, shape and hue (I'd get back to that one later), he pulled my leash toward the cache he'd promised, coming finally to a modest curtain pulled across an entrance that seemed half my height. He drew it aside and bade my entrance. I stooped and obliged, and never was a stoop so rewarded. The trove of splendid fabrics far exceeded my most jaded expectations, rows and rows of antique fabric documents and fragments folded meticulously on ancient shelves as crooked and bent as the wily proprietor, all arranged to a logic only he could navigate. Even among the embarrassment of possibilities, my eye landed on the rolled edge of an embroidered turquoise silk. Unfolded, it stole my breath—appliquéd with cinnabar and ochre crescents that tendrilled and curled around bits of Bedouin silver in some wild amoebic do-si-do. Others were found, and deals were made and sealed with hot and sugary mint tea; but that specific piece of fabric was the one that haunted my dreams that night as I fell to blissful slumber among the minarets.

Cacao Vine

The old cocoa tin on the shelf of my grandmother's pantry was a ruse. Almost a century had passed since its mottled interior had held the sweet brown powder. The acrid smell of rolled bills and heavy coins mixed oddly with a lingering chocolate scent, because that's where Nettie kept her secret stash (of money, of course). When the neighboring farmer delivered the fresh country butter pressed in a round wooden mold and wrapped in waxed paper, the tin came down from the shelf, as it did when we were going into town for an ice cream cone or when we kids needed "pocket money" for our trip back home. I think I was the only grandchild that liked the pretty little orange box and its viney decoration even more than its contents. The bittersweet color of the box itself provided strong contrast to the graphic tones of the label and floral ornamentation, the latter executed in an almost scientific fashion, illustrating the "specimen" of the cacao plant as it grew naturally in its tropical homeland. How exotic the broad-veined leaves and the nubby cacao pods, filled with the beans that provided the powder, must have seemed on the shelf of the nineteenth-century general store where her grandmother bought the tin. The pattern on the box seems exotic to me even now, perhaps more so for the generations of memory and familiarity that it represents. Years later, when Nettie passed forever to her final reward, that modest little touchstone became my link to our past.

—Barry Dixon

Inspiration comes from

our life experiences, touchstones that evoke treasured memories, and this collage pays homage to some of Barry's favorites. A whimsical bronze frog candlestick from his grandparents inspired the bronze tones of "Voyage" bullion fringe he designed for Vervain. The magical world of an Arthur Rackham illustration inspired Barry for two different executions: spider webs and grasses led to his "Papillion" printed linen; the mottled browns, maizes and yellow bronzes of quail eggs inspired his striped "Eurthymic" trim for Vervain.

Design Exclusively Screen Printed for *Verrain®* Up →

BARRY DIXON

"TALEMBAR"© An Original

Introduction

Barry Dixon Inspirations really began before our first book, *Barry Dixon Interiors* (2008) had even been finished. Barry had done so many exciting projects that we knew a second book would be needed. So, while we were wrapping up our first volume, we began compiling lists and discussing how to approach a second. We wanted it to complement the first but have a slightly different focus. And as all of these homes are meant to inspire, to provide fresh new ideas and generate enthusiasm about the creative process of good design, we chose our title to reflect this.

One of the most enjoyable parts of writing the book was visiting the individual homes. We traveled around the country from Corinth, Mississippi, an historic antebellum town in the Deep South, to a high-rise apartment in Chicago with sweeping views of downtown and Lake Michigan. And I learned something new with each project, whether it was the history of the Homestead Spa in Virginia or ways in which sustainable green materials become good and relevant design. Each and every home in the book shows a unique challenge and Barry's inspirational solutions: a French chateau on a lake in North Carolina that began as a storehouse of unmatched architectural salvage transformed into a coherent whole; a dark and narrow nineteenth-century row house in the nation's capitol opened to light and modern living for a young family with children; a tired beach house perched on the sand dunes of Delaware's Eastern Shore given a new lease on life by bringing the outdoors inside with the colors of the sea and sunset.

This book is about inspiration, where it comes from and how to translate it into good design. I hope that we stimulate each reader to take away some of Barry's tips and ideas for their own homes. And that, after all, is what inspiration is about.

—Brian Coleman

Personal Inspirations
FROM BARRY'S OWN COLLECTIONS

HUNT-THEMED rondels of hounds and their quarry animals and game found on a set of Aesthetic-period brown and white transferware were Barry's inspiration for his "Warrenton Toile," *above left*.

THE CLASSIC fretwork pattern found on the rim of nineteenth-century brown and white English transferware platters gave Barry the inspiration for this trim for Vervain, which he translated into velvet with metal and cotton with hemp, *above right*.

THE CORNER cartouches on a pair of vintage embroidered cotton sateen portieres that originally hung in Cliveden's drawing room gave Barry the inspiration for his "Cliveden" damask, which he reinterpreted in silk on a plain ground for a more modern appeal, *facing*.

AN OLD MOROCCAN
tooled leather bin inspired
Barry's "Medina" Vervain
chenille, seen here in wheat,
pumpkin and cerulean
blue colorways, *left*.

INSPIRATION took
flight in Barry's "Papillion,"
a printed linen that was
inspired by more English
transferware and vintage
studies of butterflies, *facing*.

"PEPPER PODS,"
a printed linen Barry
designed for Vervain, was
based on eighteenth-
century botanical prints of
the plants and their seeds.

A PAINTED ITALIAN CHAIR found at an antiques fair inspired Barry's "Oatlands" chair, which was reinterpreted without the nailhead-trimmed, upholstered backrest, *facing*. THE INTERLOCKING G-RING design of an antique Italian chair found in Charlottesville, Virginia, inspired Barry's "Albemarle" chair, which he updated and made more comfortable with a padded seat and back, *above*.

Cottage Modern
AT BETHANY BEACH

COLOR WAS STOLEN FROM THE OUTSIDE ELEMENTS –THE SEA, THE SKY . . . EVENING BLUES, LAVENDERS, PURPLES AND GRAYS . . .

The cottage's location was perfect, just yards off the Atlantic Ocean on Delaware's sunny Bethany Beach. The owners had been vacationing here for years and loved the simplicity of life at the shore, a stroll along the water's edge and a good book being all that was needed for a relaxing afternoon. But the house itself, built in the '80s, was cramped, dark and increasingly dated; it needed to be modernized with sensitivity, keeping in mind that it was, after all, still a modest bungalow on the beach.

AN ECLECTIC assortment of found objects and antiques add to the beach cottage charm—a giant, resin clamshell contrasts with a fine Regency-period music stand that displays *Introspection,* an oil painting by celebrated Virginia artist Charlie Westbrook. The nineteenth-century Swedish tall case clock was found at Gore Dean Antiques. Barry designed the open-back "Roseanne" bench that is covered in Rogers and Goffigon's pale lavender linen.

Barry had designed two other residences for the couple and knew what they needed—a place to entertain frequent family and guests, interiors that were open and welcoming, filled with color and light, a home that reflected the ocean and brought its beauty back inside.

Initial plans were to substantially expand the small house, but a review of building ordinances revealed that new oceanside construction was now prohibited. So, rather than lose the idyllic setting on top of the dunes, working with architect Chris Pattey, Barry kept within the original footprint of the cottage, modernizing it and in the process making the small rooms seem larger, all the while maximizing the mesmerizing views. Work began on the second level of the three-story residence, the core of the home. Walls were removed to create one open and welcoming interior for living, dining and entertaining, a comfortable place to just relax and watch the pounding surf. Original pilings and supports could not be removed and so were celebrated, instead, as an integral part of the design. Deftly placed mirrors, sandblasted glass panels and walls, and a new bank of windows on the south façade flooded the room with light and lent to the illusion of space and height. Reclaimed lumber floors, clarified with a simple bleach wash, were laid on the diagonal pointing toward the ocean, subtly reinforcing and uniting the open interior with the outdoors.

CLARENCE HOUSE'S "Dundee" drapery in a relaxing "Flint" colorway is combined with walls upholstered in granite "Tumbled Steer" grained vinyl from Valtekz's in the masculine guest study. Note that the curtains extend to the ceiling for an illusion of height. The "Alan" sofa was designed by Barry for Tomlinson and covered with Myung Jin's soft woven "Quail Creek," its bottom scalloped edge undulating like a rolling wave.

The "Hallings" secretary by Thomas O'Brien (for Hickory Chair) has an ivory finish with a leather desktop. A "Felix Round" side table from Julian Chichester in a bronze finish with a shagreen inset emphasizes the machine age modern appeal, *facing*.

TALL SIDE PANELS on the "Caribou" chairs undulate like cresting waves on the seashore. Note the pewter tacks that subtly define their outlines.

SOLID BLOCKS OF COLOR WERE USED FOR THE FURNITURE TO FURTHER EMULATE THE OUTDOORS, AND TOO-BUSY PATTERNS WERE SCRUPULOUSLY AVOIDED.

A modern industrial focus was used to bring the house out of its '80s time warp: the original pilings were sheathed in gunmetal gray riveted steel columns, and the steel was repeated as the fireplace surround. A modern galley kitchen, using only green and carbon-neutral materials from SeiMatic, replaced the original worn cabinets; new cylindrical stainless steel stove vents suspended from the ceiling are reminiscent of smoke stacks on an ocean liner.

Color was stolen from the outside elements—the sea, the sky and the ever-shifting dunes. The colors of the morning— bright, crisp whites and sandy creams that turn hot white with the noonday sun were combined with evening blues, lavenders, purples and grays, the spectrum of the ocean's light as it recedes into twilight.

Barry was careful to use solid blocks of color for the furniture to further emulate the outdoors, and too-busy patterns were scrupulously avoided. "Venue," a simple, cotton velvet from Vervain, was selected in two colorways for living room upholstery: stormy sky blue (#40) for a pair of "Caribou" armchairs from Ironies, and sunset lavender (#32) for a cushy "Basse Terre" Christian Liaigre sofa from Holly Hunt set in front of the glass doors to the terrace. The room was anchored with a circular sea grass rug banded with Vervain's textured velvet "Persian Cloud," its round shape lending a subtle counterpoint and helping visually expand the rectangular room.

A pair of iconic 1940s carved knot chairs from Gore Dean Antiques were recovered with a natural cream linen from Vervain, while Glant's "Couture Herringbone" textured linen in an organic lilac was chosen for the "Sargasso" ottoman Barry designed to encircle one of the steel-encased pilings in the center of the room. "Hendricks" demilune consoles constructed of cerused oak with limestone tops (created for Tomlinson) were set on either side of the fireplace for an Arts and Crafts simplicity and honesty of design.

A PILLOW FROM ANKASA
in a natural linen with bone appliqués rests on the vintage, rope-carved chair in the living room that is covered with a natural linen from Vervain, *left*.

WHILE THE CEILINGS are just nine feet tall, the main living room seems much larger by clever use of color and light. Walls and ceiling are painted with Farrow & Ball "Elephant's Breath" to help unify the room's many planes. The steel encasing the pilings was used as the fireplace surround, pulling the riveted, gunmetal gray material to the back for balance; the television is cleverly camouflaged by its similar graphite colorway. A double layer of curtains helps diffuse and filter the light: netted "Casement" curtains in cream from Donghia overlay "Brussels Glaze" sheers by Henry Calvin in "Natural," *above*.

No detail was too small—even furniture height was carefully considered to maximize the views throughout the room; seating was made three to four inches taller on the far end of the room so that the views could still be appreciated from across the large space. Walls and ceiling were painted with Farrow & Ball "Elephant's Breath," a warm and neutral cohesive gray, to help tie the elements of the room together.

SOLID BLOCKS OF COLORS are used to keep the room simple, foregoing patterns that might detract from the striking views outdoors. The oval, polished pewter cocktail table centers the seating area that includes an "Ellipse Chaise" designed by Barry on the right.

To diffuse the light and add a golden glow throughout the day, the windows were layered with two sets of open mesh curtains, "Brussels Glaze" sheers from Henry Calvin overlaid with open net panels of Donghia's cream jute-and-cotton "Casement." As the sun rises in the morning and streams into the room, light and color indoors and out merge together and the room expands into the sky and ocean beyond.

PURPOSELY SKEWED PERSPECTIVES

AN INDUSTRIAL IRON RAILING rests on the glass wall leading to the lower level and adds to the modern, machine age essence, *above*. **A SOLID WALL** under the staircase was replaced with glass to illuminate the lower stairwell; note the combination of purposefully skewed perspectives—curves with sharp angles, new with old that gives the interior an integrated but very personal appeal. The amber resin table is from Oly, *facing*.

SLEEK, SMOKE STACK-LIKE vents from SieMatic lend the kitchen a maritime appeal, while the sandblasted glass cupboard seems as much an abstract artwork as it does storage. Glass domes of sea urchins from Natural Curiosities and pewter candlesticks from Barneys add an eclectic and personal touch.

A simple open galley kitchen was placed at the north end of the room for ease of preparation and serving guests. Everything was carefully tailored for a modern refinement—the refrigerator, pantry and microwave were hidden behind textured wood panels inset into one wall, storage garages were constructed to conceal appliances inside the cabinets, and even the granite countertops were thinly cut to enable them to be meticulously inset into the counters for a more streamlined look. Ordinary wall-hung cupboards were eschewed to open the space to light and the views; a single sandblasted glass cabinet was hung on one wall as an accent, much like a piece of art. A bar-height, round bamboo-and-stainless steel table from Lowenstein, polished nickel bar stools from Casamidy, and a globe overhead constructed of coconut shells added to the kitchen's sleek, machine age ambience, the added height of the stools giving their occupants better advantage of the view.

THE GALLEY KITCHEN was designed with kitchen consultant Jonas Carnemark using SieMatic carbon-neutral and green products. The refrigerator and microwave are hidden behind textured wood panels inset into the wall, and an antique rooster weather vane from Gore Dean Antiques playfully anchors the end of the counter.

LOOKING ACROSS THE main floor toward the open dining area, an unusual chandelier of recycled glass orbs from Four Hands hangs above the Ironies dining table. Barry designed the "Sargasso" ottoman in two halves to fit around the steel column. A circular sea grass rug from Floor Gallery echoes the curves of the room's furnishings and helps mitigate the room's angles. The "Caribou" chair from Ironies is covered in Vervain's blue cotton velvet "Venue."

A
n open dining room

adjacent to the kitchen was centered on an organic "St. Denis" table from Ironies, its stone top inset with fossils, anchored by a striking pendant light above of recycled glass orbs, much like fishing floats washed up by the sea. Iconic Frances Elkins game chairs (based on classic card room chairs she designed in 1937) were set around the table for comfortable seating. Storage was kept simple and straightforward: an open-shelf etagere was placed in front of a window for easy access to dinnerware; ocean light streams inside and highlights the stacks of rich, amethyst-colored Fiestaware plates and dishes on its shelves.

AN ODEGARD "CORNET" console with a sterling silver base and amethyst-colored stone top rests next to the dining table for service and displays found objects and art: a nineteenth-century seascape (suspended from the ceiling by a nearly invisible chain), a lamp from Stephan Olivier fashioned from a piece of gnarled yew wood, a machinery cog, clusters of seed pods from a palm, *facing*.

THE OLY HEADBOARD in the guest bedroom is covered in simple raffia, a good complement for the mulberry tones of the room. Samuel and Sons trim used to cover the coverlet's seams also facilitates centering it when making the bed. A custom made Mitchell Yanosky "Hatbox Parsons Table" is covered in lavender linen that has been lacquered for the effect of a textured wood surface, *facing*.

TEXTURE, COLOR and pattern are skillfully combined in the guest bedroom—a resin vase from Oly holds seasonal flowers that echo the damask design of Home Couture "Prague" upholstered onto the walls. An "Anni" mirror from Julian Chichester reflects coastal wildlife, including birds and starfish, *left*.

A pair of bedrooms

on the west side of the second level facing the inland marsh flats was made into a cozy and intimate guest suite, its rooms connected by a guest bath defined by translucent, rolling glass doors, which provide privacy but do not block the ambient light. The bedroom was enveloped in "Prague," a soft, mulberry-colored washed linen from Home Couture, which was used to cover not only the walls but the ceiling as well. Its bold, stylized damask pattern gives the small room unexpected drama and actually makes it seem larger and more important. The floor was deliberately left bare to balance and give relief to the upholstered ceiling, creating an overall effect almost as if the room had been turned upside down, as if one were swimming down into an underwater grotto. Additional tricks to visually expand the small room include hiding the bed frame within the folds of the overhanging mulberry coverlet so it seems to

be floating above the floor, and incorporating a special drapery rod system ("Ripple Fold Track") that mounts directly into the ceiling and glides the curtains on ball bearings, making the walls appear taller. As the main view was through a side window, traditional room arrangement was not followed; rather, the bed was nestled in the center of the room, in front of a viewless window in a curved niche created by the draperies hung from the ceiling. Guests can now pleasantly wake up to the golden sunlight as it rises over the sand dunes and ocean and streams inside.

The adjoining guest sitting room was kept quiet and masculine, befitting its use as a study. Its walls were upholstered in Valtekz's granite-colored "Tumbled Steer" grained cowhide vinyl, set off with a handsome pewter nail-head trim, while Ralph Lauren "Ambassador Sterling" pewter-gray metallic paint on the ceiling lent an industrial reference. Soft folds of Clarence House's flint-colored "Dundee" drapes framed the room, hung from the ceiling for more height and presence.

The staircase leading to the third level was given more sparkle and visual impact by hanging a collection of circular mirrors made from recycled metal barrel rims on the ascending wall.

SPARKLE AND VISUAL IMPACT

MIRRORS INSET INTO RECYCLED barrel rims reflect the light back into the staircase;
the painting at the top, from Oly Studio, is inspired by original Audubon studies.

THE MASTER BED by Calvin Klein Home looks directly out over the ocean; spread with a metallic gray linen coverlet from Glant Fabrics, the bed is upholstered in Vervain's silvery cut velvet "Venue" for a feeling of luxury. An octopus triptych by Christopher Wilcox from Natural Curiosities adds to the organic, underwater effect. Fantastic shapes and angles were purposely chosen to subtly confuse the eye and transcend the smallness of the room— sculptural floor lamps from Oly on either side of the bed, a pair of conical night stands from Ruth Livingston Studios in highly polished sycamore to contrast with the angled wooden floors.

pstairs a master suite overlooking the Atlantic was carved out of two existing bedrooms. The bedroom ceiling was opened up to the attic, where the beams were left exposed for more height and the ceiling between the beams was papered with "Sepia Quartz," a mica-encrusted, purple quartz paper from Maya Romanoff, for an underwater sparkle. Walls were painted in rich, metallic Regent "York Purple" from Ralph Lauren, making the room seem as if it were set inside a shimmering, iridescent sea shell. Hyacinth-purple, tie-died linen "Colorfield" drapery panels at the windows, by Isaac Mizrahi for S. Harris, added to the lustrous atmosphere. Industrial details were added for a more modern look—a metallic gunmetal gray column was designed to encase pipes that could not be easily moved; a riveted steel fireplace was installed across the room in a dark, gunmetal finish; and a sandblasted Bulthrup rolling glass door was hung to close off the master bath.

AN ANTIQUE STONE head
of Hermes, from Gore Dean
Antiques, centers the walk-in
shower in the master bath; a
Casamidy wire chair is covered
in Valtekz's lavender vinyl by
Celerie Kemble. Note how
the raised, slightly swaled
floor eliminates the need of
a shower curtain, *below*.

A striking, freestanding "Oval" bathtub from Waterworks was installed, placed in the center of the room so bathers can look directly out to the ocean as they soak in the tub. The floor and walls were tiled in reflective silver and gray slate mosaic tiles, and with Ralph Lauren's rich Regent "Manchester Purple" paint on the ceiling and silvery gray Donghia sheers billowing at the windows, the overall effect is almost like lounging on the ocean floor. A custom-designed set of open-mesh shelved consoles with reflective onyx counters on either side of the room were made to hold towels and toiletries. (The metal, claw-footed legs, cleverly left hollow, hide the electrical cords inside.)

THE MASTER BATH
looks out towards the
ocean and is centered
on an "Oval" soaking
tub from Waterworks.
Mosaic stone floors by
Architectural Ceramics
and "Opus" faucet sets
by Waterworks in a
smooth, satin nickel finish
add to the watery effect.
A pair of commodes
designed by Barry for
Averett Metal Works hold
towels from Waterworks
in rosy "Quartz" and
silvery "Platinum"; their
alabaster tops are lit by
Egg lamps from Jamie
Young. The semainier
on the left, from Julian
Chichester, is finished in
silvery metallic tones.

BARRY USED his playful "Corset Chair" from Tomlinson for the guest room. The chair is covered in "Roji Silk," a watery, celadon silk chenille from Glant, and accented with Samuel and Sons trim.

The guest room's drapery panels are made in aquamarine "Newport," a crimped, watery woven silk-and-paper fabric from Pierre Frey, and accented with trim from Fabricut.

Another guest suite

on the opposite end of the third floor was designed in a palette of watery blues, brackish greens and golds, reflecting the color of the inland marshes outside. Walls were painted in Farrow & Ball "Green Blue," and the room was centered on an open, four-poster "Sutton Place" bed from EFLM in recycled, cerused walnut. Silk "aquamarina" draperies from Pierre Frey, a lamp made of coral, and a series of "Circle Cool" oil paintings in sea green, surf blue and sunset yellow from Oly Studios were hung tightly across the wall—all adding to the marshlands mood. The adjoining bath was designed to complement the bedroom, whose walls were tiled in Waterworks' slag glass "Repose Tile" in the Clearwater colorway (jade, inky blue, and deep aquatic blue-green), run horizontally rather than vertically for a striking, brick-like effect.

Drawing inspiration from its seaside surroundings for everything from the color palettes to the furnishings to the orientation of the rooms, Barry successfully updated this modest beach bungalow, transforming it into an open, modern home, at one with its setting and squarely in the comfort of the twenty-first century.

THE UPSTAIRS GUEST bedroom is centered on a "Sutton Place" open, four-poster bed from EFLM that is made from recycled, cerused walnut. The walls are painted with Farrow & Ball "Green Blue." A "Clawfoot" desk from Design Workshop, for correspondence or a laptop, is set in the corner of the room, *facing*.

PALETTE OF WATERY BLUES

OIL PAINTINGS FROM OLY STUDIO, including the *Circle Cool* series and swans in a marsh, emphasize the wetlands atmosphere, *facing*. The adjoining guest bath is clad in vertical rows of slag glass "Repose Tile" from Waterworks to complement the brackish greens of the guest room. **A MIRROR CUSTOM DESIGNED** by Barry from Avery Fine Arts, a vitreous china pedestal sink in ice gray from Kohler, and graphite metal sconces from Robert Abbey reinforce the slick, industrial ambiance, *above*.

Barry's Inspiration**&**Tips

When a room's view is exceptional, avoid use of busy fabrics to keep the eye's focus on the outdoors.

Consider seating heights— subtly raised heights of just three to four inches enhance access to views from across a room.

Keep kitchen wall cabinets to a minimum for more light and a feeling of spaciousness.

Hide unsightly electrical cords within or behind a table leg for a cleaner, less cluttered look.

An overscaled pattern in a small room gives it unexpected drama and makes it seem larger.

Chateau Chic
IN NORTH CAROLINA

THE COLORS OF THE LAKESIDE SETTING—AZURE
BLUES AND WATERY GREENS—WERE BROUGHT BACK
INSIDE, TYING THE HOME TO ITS SETTING.

When the owners called Barry they were in a panic. Midway through construction, they had fired their architect and designer and didn't know where to turn. Granted, their project was unusual: after having collected a warehouse full of architectural antiques from France, they decided to build a chateau-style home and had found the perfect site—a wooded glen on the edge of a picturesque lake in North Carolina. Always ready for a challenge, Barry agreed to the project, realizing his

A CUSTOM SOCIABLE is upholstered in Quadrille's Dijon-gold "Venezia" linen velvet and accented with brass nail head trim in a floral motif, echoing the curvilinear floral vine motif of the stairway's iron railings.

A ROSE TARLOW infirmary chair in the family room rests next to an antique, carved and gilded table, *left*.

BARRY BEGAN BY CONDUCTING AN EXTENSIVE INVENTORY: EVERY ITEM WAS PHOTOGRAPHED, MEASURED AND DOCUMENTED SO THAT THE PROJECT COULD BE ORGANIZED IN A SEAMLESS AND COHESIVE MANNER.

task would be much like assembling a giant jigsaw puzzle. He had to somehow integrate 72 odd doors, scores of windows, antique stone arches and flooring, three eighteenth-century paneled rooms, and stone fireplaces—one large enough to walk into. Chimney pots and chandeliers, a vintage elevator, even a large built-in wall clock all had to be brought together to form a coherent interior, one with the Gallic character and charm of a medieval French chateau combined with the livability of a twenty-first-century home for a modern American family.

Barry began by conducting an extensive inventory: every item was photographed, measured and documented so that the project could be organized in a seamless and cohesive manner. Working with Charlotte architect Mike Doyne, the scale of many of the rooms was adjusted in an effort to make them smaller and more inviting; stone walls were given warmth with thickly lined floor-length portieres and draperies, and the rooms were filled with comfortable and invitingly upholstered furnishings. The colors of the lakeside setting—azure blues and watery greens—were brought back inside, tying the home to its setting.

The dramatic entrance to the castle is through nineteenth-century, fourteen-foot arched glass doors that open into a two-story stone hall with a sweeping, curved limestone staircase. The foyer was designed as both an entrance hall and a salon, grand but humanized with soft furnishings and finishes. The walls were textured in a neutral ombre finish (the colors gradually shifting from soft sands to light, paper bag browns as they rise to the ceiling) to emulate the ancient stone floors. The space's formality is accented with an eighteenth-century cut crystal-and-iron chandelier hung in the center. Occasional chairs include a pair of eighteenth-century French fauteuils upholstered in Gisbert Rentmeister's organic wool-and-cotton "Mais" and Barry's quatrefoil, open-back "Roseanne" side chairs upholstered in Fortuny's yellow and silvery gold cotton "Campanelle"; more Fortuny was used for sweeping portieres hung on either side of foyer niches.

PORTIERES OF
Scalamandré "Monochromo" lampas add intimacy to the dining room and complement the soft blue and olive tones of the room, *facing*.

A GRACEFUL ARCH
marks the entrance into the dining room from the adjacent foyer. Ceiling moldings were added to the antique French wall panels to give them a more finished look. The trumeau oil landscapes are original to the eighteenth-century paneling, *right*.

A graceful archway leads into the dining room. Walled with ornately carved eighteenth-century panels from a long-gone Loire Valley estate, with original painted landscapes still intact in the upper inserts, this room is centered on a magnificent three-tiered iron, crystal and gilt wood Italian chandelier hung from the sixteen-foot ceiling. A long walnut dining table from New Classics anchors the room underneath. Seating was broken up with a combination of two different sets of chairs for more character and appeal: Julia Gray's "Louis XVI" carved chairs were mixed with a dozen nineteenth-century French oval-backed dining chairs upholstered in Fortuny's silvery and gold "Granada"; a chartreuse mohair velvet was used on the backs of all of the chairs to unify the ensemble. The oval ceiling was painted with Farrow & Ball "Sky Blue" to complement portieres and window draperies of Scalamandré "Monochromo" lampas in shades of pear, olive and sky blue. Intimacy in the large room was introduced by a second, smaller dining table set in the bowed window alcove, a perfect spot for smaller dinner parties, desserts or a cup of afternoon tea.

A JULIA GRAY "Louis XVI" dining room chair upholstered in a gauffraged velvet from Northcroft rests in front of built-in china and silver cabinets, *above left*.

ORIGINAL ANTIQUE DOOR HARDWARE highlights the polychrome and gilded accents on the panels, *above right*.

AN EIGHTEEN-FOOT-TALL china cabinet is filled with eighteenth-century French dinnerware and Ming Dynasty muses, *left*.

A THREE-TIER GILT wood, crystal and iron chandelier is centered over the oval walnut dining table from New Classics. Fortuny "Granada" was used to upholster the seat and front of the oval chair backs, then combined with a chartreuse mohair velvet, which was used on the backs of all the dining room chairs to unify the ensemble. Blue glass hurricanes on the table echo the inside of the cabinets painted Farrow & Ball "Sky Blue," *facing*.

The kitchen was designed for professional cooking with two separate islands—one marble topped for pastry and dessert preparation, the second a mesquite chopping island with a sink and drainboard. Walls were finished in a stone glaze to complement others throughout the home, and cabinets were given washes in buttermilk and sage green. A late-nineteenth-century wrought-iron French chandelier fitted with S-hooks doubles as a handy overhead rack for pots and cooking utensils. Barry added simple Arts and Crafts brackets of quarter-sawn lime oak to anchor the pecky cypress beams on the ceiling. The adjoining conservatory off the kitchen was designed with the appeal of an English garden room, a simple spot for a cup of coffee and reading the morning paper while looking over the lake. A round antique French slate garden table is set for comfortable dining with Formation's lattice-backed chairs upholstered in Sanderson "Standen," a pale sunflower linen-and-cotton weave; a concave "Elyse" corner cabinet from Dennis & Leen is nestled in the corner. Panels of Bergamo organic "Butterfly" linen in maize, leaf green and vermilion filter the morning light as it streams through the glass walls and ceiling.

THE HEART OF THE kitchen is a brass-and-copper La Cornue gas range with a hammered steel-and-brass hood that Barry designed. Inspired by Maxfield Parrish illustrations, the concept was brought to life by Kelly Metalworks. A mosaic backsplash in a basket weave pattern carries the texture of the reclaimed stone floors .onto the walls. The butler's pantry is glimpsed to the right, *facing*.

ANTIQUES AND ARCHITECTURE

THE KITCHEN WAS DESIGNED with Premier Cabinets and finished in shades of textured stone to complement the floors, but with warmer tones of sage green, ivory and soft buttermilk. A pair of islands, one with a marble top for pastry and desserts, the second with a mesquite surface for chopping, make food prep efficient. A vintage French chandelier from Amy Perlin doubles as a handy pot rack overhead, *above*. **THE GLASS CONSERVATORY OPENS** off the kitchen at the back of the house, facing the lake. The antique French slate table centers the space. A Chinoiserie-style iron lantern overhead, from Niermann Weeks, conjures the theme of a garden folly, *facing*.

A MAGNIFICENT
repurposed limestone
fireplace found in France
is the hub of the family
room. Walls were textured
in shades of ochre and
stone to complement the
fireplace, and comfortable
furnishings include a pair
of Barry's "Sawyer" sofas
from Tomlinson and a
Baker chair and ottoman.
A plasma screen TV
is artfully concealed in
Barry's goatskin-covered
"Simone" cabinet. Note
the salvaged French doors
that add to the room's
character and charm

A massive seven-teenth-century limestone fire-place from the Loire Valley in France anchors the family room. Overscaled furnishings were used to humanize the grand scale and make the room more intimate and approachable: a pair of Bar-ry's "Sawyer" sofas upholstered in Rose Tarlow's brandy-colored "Matchsticks" velvet were set with a pair of Robert Kuo bronze tables from McGuire in front, along with a "Tuileries" chair and ottoman from Baker, covered in Sanderson's "Petersham Rib," a casual ribbed velvet in harvest gold, wheat and ochre. A mas-sive three-tier "Marcella" bronze chandelier from Ironware Inter-national helped visually lower the room's twenty-two-foot ceiling.

A SOFT "MOSELLE" chaise from Edward Ferrell and Lewis Mittman, covered in Scalamandré "Bantry House" linen, nestles in the corner beneath a collection of eighteenth-century copperplate engravings on the wall above, *facing*.

GLIMPSED THRU THE wrought-iron balcony, a guest bedroom is centered on a custom headboard outlined with polished brass tacks. Appliquéd Ankasa bed linens complement the headboard. A nineteenth-century

Barbizon school oil hangs above a table desk from Hickory Chair, *above*.

A dramatic, sweeping staircase curves up to the second-story gallery and the bedroom suites, the floral silhouette of its curvilinear railings based on an architectural fragment of balcony railing found in France. More architectural salvage is incorporated throughout: a guest bedroom features a built-in armoire made from sal-vaged doors, painted in Farrow & Ball "New White," a pleasant complement to the room's powdery "Sky Blue" walls. A palette of French blues and purples is continued with a turquoise nineteenth-century serpentine desk at the window. A Julia Gray "Cane" bed is invitingly covered with a quilted nineteenth-century "Boutis" coverlet from France.

ANOTHER GUEST
bedroom is painted with
Farrow & Ball "Sky Blue" on
the walls, with added accents
of lavenders and creams
lending sophisticated French
charm. Hancock and Moore's

"Desmond" bergère and
ottoman is upholstered in
Boussac Fadani's amethyst-
hued "Lucinda," a woven
damask, while a turquoise
nineteenth-century French
desk rests in front of the

window. Every door in the
room is a repurposed antique,
tied together with Farrow &
Ball "New White," *above*.

THE CURVES of a guest
bath's "Kallista" claw-foot tub
are accented by the gracefully
curved archways. Reclaimed
stone was accented with
tiles to carry the theme from
the rest of the house.

A COLLECTION OF found treasures rests on the desk: a tooled-leather-and-silver antique box, turquoise gourd vases, drawings of butterflies and caterpillars from Natural Curiosities.

A LOUIS FERRELL and Edward Ferrell loveseat covered in Old World Weaver "Cabana" stripe rests at the foot of the bed. The walls are covered in Tyler Graphic's "Cedar" linen. Iron stair balustrades were made into bedside lamps, echoing the iron four-poster bed.

NINETEENTH-CENTURY engravings of eggs echo the colors of the room—soft taupe, wheat, and salmon. An eighteenth-century glass bottle filled with yarrow rests on the painted chest.

A rchitectural salvage was again highlighted in a second guest bedroom. Cypress ceiling beams were given just a light coat of wax to highlight their grain, and furnishings were found that emphasized natural elements: a four-poster bed from Ironies, covered with an antique Suzani found in Istanbul, is juxtaposed with an antique straw Moroccan rug across the room. A seating area in front of the French doors and balcony is set with a pair of wingback chairs from Formations, here upholstered in Pollack's crème brûlée "Twister."

FRENCH CHATEAU INSPIRATION

AN OPEN, EUROPEAN-STYLE guest bath can be closed off with leather screens. Centered on a gleaming "Kallista" copper tub, the room was inspired by a similar bath the owners saw in Provence. The terra-cotta tile floor was carried up a third of the wall for the appeal of an ancient Roman bath. **IN THE ADJOINING GUEST BEDROOM,** vintage materials are used to lend French countryside charm, with an open iron "Branwen" bed from Ironies and an antique tooled-leather Spanish screen covering the back of the room.

A curvilinear scrolled
niche was created behind the leather-upholstered French bed in the master bedroom for more dramatic focus and accented with luxurious seafoam green "Organza Leaf" taffeta panels from Myung Jin. Inspired by the lake, a watery colored mural was commissioned for the walls; the lakeside colors were continued in the upholstery fabrics, including Cowtan & Tout's aqua silk "Castile Scallop" for a pair of "Barrymore" chairs set in the window bay. A collection of framed eighteenth-century pressed seaweed specimens inspired the color of the adjoining master bath, whose Venetian plaster walls and ceiling were polished in a rich aqua-toned finish.

A NICHE WAS created to make the bed a focal point in the master bedroom. The walls are finished in a watery, misty, celadon mural by Warnock Studios, and the colors of the lake are emphasized with sea foam green "Organza Leaf" taffeta panels from Myung Jin hung behind the bed. An organic round rug in an Arts and Crafts motif of leaves and vines banded with cocoa-colored leather emphasizes the outdoors, *above*.

A PAIR OF "Barrymore" lounge chairs upholstered in Zoffany "Linen Press" flanks the antique marble fireplace in the master bedroom, *facing*.

WATERY BLUE BORROWED LIGHT

BARRY'S "MARIA" sofa upholstered in Donghia "Fiesole" chenille is set in the deep window bay of the master bedroom. The celadon-colored sheer draperies are appliquéd with bands of antique Chinese silk for the elegant sophistication of a haute couture gown, *facing*. **SPACIOUS AND FILLED** with light, the master bath's Venetian plaster walls are infused with Farrow & Ball watery blue "Borrowed Light," its color complemented by the café au lait tumbled marble floor. His and hers vanities on custom iron bases are lit by sparkling Venetian glass sconces from Marvin Alexander. A wall of curved glass surrounds an exposed steam shower in the center of the room.

WITH CAREFUL ORGANIZATION AND PLANNING. BARRY ACCOMPLISHED A COMPLEX AND SEEMINGLY IMPOSSIBLE TASK, TURNING A DISPARATE ASSEMBLAGE OF ARCHITECTURAL ARTIFACTS INTO A COHERENT, UNIFIED AND INVITING HOME.

An upstairs study was nestled in the domed turret, its entrance marked by weighty columns of pinion stone, which is repeated in the deep arched window surrounds. Centered on a carved Louis XV limestone chimneypiece, the room is a convenient place to read and relax with Brunschwig & Fils' lounge chair and ottoman, "upholstered in "Hinsdale Woven Stripe" from Kathryn Ireland." An iron Louis XIV chandelier from Dennis & Leen echoes the curves of the fireplace.

A LIBRARY CORNER in the family room has a curved bibliotheque to break up the angularity of the room. Fortuny portieres soften the space and lend a note of fluidity, *above*.

A SHARED UPSTAIRS study at the top of the turret has French doors opening to a balcony overlooking the lake. The room is furnished for reading and games with Barry's "Zeus" ottoman, a Brunschwig & Fils cushy lounge chair and ottoman, and an elegantly curved bench from Amy Howard in front of the fireplace. Uncovered iron casement windows let the light from the lake stream inside, *facing*.

Barry's Tips

Soften hard surfaces, such as stone, visually and acoustically with soft, forgiving fabrics—portieres, curtains and upholstered pieces.

Give a simple or underscaled bed drama and scale with a niche and/or curtains behind.

Break up a dining table's formality with different chairs, subtly coordinating them with their upholstery.

In kitchens or rooms with a lot of woodwork, use a variety of complementary stains and finishes for more visual interest.

Bring depth and perspective to an ordinary room with custom murals and finishes. Remember that talented artisans are a designer's best friend.

Stately Living
IN NASHVILLE

BARRY WAS CAREFUL TO RESPECT THE HOME'S
ARCHITECTURE AND SENSE OF FORMALITY, UPDATING
SPACES IN A SEAMLESS AND WELCOMING MANNER.

The owner had grown up in this stately Nashville home, a 1920s antebellum shaded by massive elm and walnut trees, and acquired it some years into adulthood. The house had good bones with the best of Southern neoclassical architecture: a broad fanlight above the front door, an attractive staircase in the front hall, columns, pilasters and handsome molding. But the early-twentieth-century rooms were too small for his growing family and comfortable entertaining.

MEMENTOS MAKE the
entry personal and welcoming.
The garden gate console
table holds a lamp with the
look of an ancient marble
balustrade. Barry's "Oatlands"
chair is covered with Fortuny's
"Canestrelli" fabric.

ROOMS WERE OPENED UP TO CREATE EASY CIRCULATION BETWEEN THE MAIN AREAS— RECEPTION, DINING AND LIVING QUARTERS. THE HANDSOME ORIGINAL STAIRCASE IN THE ENTRY WAS CAREFULLY PRESERVED, SETTING A GRACIOUS NOTE OF NEOCLASSIC FORMALITY.

Barry had designed the owner's previous home more than a decade earlier and understood the family's needs: celebrating family heritage and traditions but bringing spaces forward for an active lifestyle.

Working closely with architect Daniel Lee and the owners, Barry extended the axial lines of the house, adding wings to either end and a large, two-story living room to the back. Rooms were opened up to create easy circulation between the main areas— reception, dining and living quarters. The handsome original staircase in the entry was carefully preserved, setting a gracious note of neoclassic formality. As the original home's windows were small, light was introduced throughout with higher doors, transoms, taller windows, clerestories and skylights, along with rounded bays lined with French doors in the master suite and family room. Every major room was given at least one fireplace for cool winter nights. Landscape architect Ben Page added a new pool and a pool house, designed with glass doors that opened to the gardens, and the grounds were redesigned to integrate with the home. Furniture from the owner's previous home

was freshened and repurposed for a sense of constancy: dining chairs were reupholstered; a favorite antique French center table was given new life in the master suite; a pair of wrought-iron consoles created from salvaged garden gates were pushed together into one long table to welcome visitors in the entry. Barry was careful to respect the home's architecture and sense of formality, updating spaces in a seamless and welcoming manner.

The formal foyer set the tone for the home and was carefully conserved, its staircase, walls and columns freshened with Farrow & Ball's warm ivory "Clunch" applied in a striated finish for subtle depth. The previously mentioned console table was set with family collections and mementos for a hospitable note of familiarity and included antique glass medicine vials and historic letters from famous Americans such as Thomas Jefferson and Andrew Jackson. A collection of eighteenth-century Italian engravings by Claude Lorraine of architectural ruins was hung above to subtly reinforce the classical theme.

TONES OF SILVER and gold shimmer in the front parlor with metallized Gracie Art Deco wall panels. The darkly stained original Greek Revival mantel is lightened with Farrow & Ball "Clunch." The seagrass carpet is bordered in Stroheim & Romann's gold "James" velvet to underscore the room's yellow accents. A center table with an acanthus leaf base and top inlaid with walnut and olive wood rests in front of Barry's "Maria" sofa. An elegant Dessin Fournir chair is upholstered with a Quadrille fabric in gold, ivory and topaz stripes.

The original living room, directly off the foyer, was turned into an intimate reception parlor. The walls were covered in silvery gold, hand-painted Gracie panels in a scenic French Deco design. Their shimmery metallic finishes were emphasized with a silvered John Rosselli pendant ceiling light and an inlaid walnut-and-olive center table from New Classics with a striking gilded acanthus-leaf base. Golden tones were further accented with Dessin Fournir's "Elliot" bergère upholstered in Quadrille's playful "Rugantino" with stripes of ecru, gold and topaz.

While tones of gold and silver were elegantly layered together for an opulent appeal, the effect was kept from becoming overwhelming with the clean ivory palette of Farrow & Ball "Clunch" on the woodwork, along with "Knoles Spangled Bedroom," a cream-colored Zoffany woven that was used to upholster Barry's "Maria" sofa set in the window. "Fan Faliero," a Scalamandré Colony Collection silk and linen, was hung like a ball gown at the windows, crimped and gathered to further soften and envelop the room.

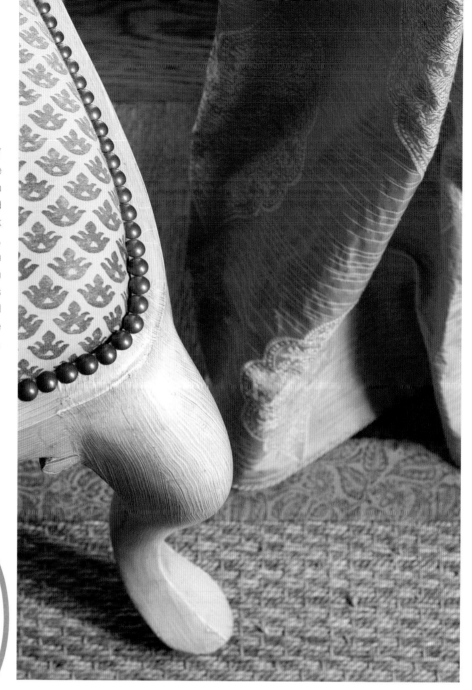

COMPLEMENTARY COLORS help make the dining room warm, inviting and cohesive: apricot silk walls and draperies, terra-cotta and cream "Canestrelli" Fortuny on the chairs, and bands of golden Townsend Leather bordering the seagrass carpet, *right*.

On the opposite side of the foyer, the original dining room was kept intact. Its intimacy was emphasized by upholstering the walls with Donghia "Bindi," a warm, almond-colored Indian patterned silk that was repeated as draperies on the windows. French doors along one wall opened the room to the gardens, and a custom quatrefoiled plaster ceiling was installed to suggest a garden trellis. The dining table was complemented by Barry's "Oatlands" dining side chairs upholstered with Fortuny's rust-and-beige "Canestrelli." A pair of "Chevalier" iron-and-wood chandeliers from Niermann Weeks, sparkling with silver and gold leaf highlights, became an elegant accent overhead.

THE DINING ROOM walls were upholstered in Donghia "Bindi," which was continued as draperies. A pearwood-and-walnut dining table from New Classics centers the room, *facing*.

A MEZZANINE on the front stairway looks over the two-story living room. Neoclassical details inspired by the original home were enlarged for a stronger impact. Symmetry is emphasized: note the interior second-story window, one of four set into each upper quadrant of the room. A "Circolo" writing table from Niermann Weeks is set with a lyre-backed "Faringale" wing chair from Rose Tarlow, here upholstered in an embroidered silk. A stone table lamp from Panache provides a classical garden accent, *facing*.

A 1920S chinoiserie floor lamp provides light next to the Panache day bed. Antique Mexican silver goblets and plates and a pair of French garden urns rest on the mantel. The burnished bronze "Burgess" firescreen is from Averett, *right*.

The rear wall of the entrance foyer was removed and a grand two-story living room created beyond. Symmetry, an important component of classic design, was enhanced by twin fireplaces on either end, along with neoclassic columns, pilasters and molding details repeated from the original home but on a grander, more striking scale. French doors capped by a central fanlight let light pour in throughout the day, with embroidered silk draperies from Taffard Fabrics softening the sunlight. The romantic appeal of the Italian countryside was introduced with grisaille panels of Zuber's "Pay-

sage Italien," a hand-printed 1912 design, above either fireplace. Anchoring the room underneath was a custom Oushak-style carpet woven in a muted palette of salmon, apricot, pale honey and pistachio for the look of a delightfully faded antique. Comfortable furnishings were selected and arranged in groups for easy conversation—a pair of Barry's "Alan" scalloped-edge sofas covered in Myung Jin's cinnamon wool "Tex-scape" flanking one fireplace, an inviting "Palermo" daybed from Panache upholstered in a cheerful coral cotton velvet from Vervain in front of the other. Barry's translucent wire

THE LIVING ROOM is centered on Barry's "Obelisk" metal mesh pedestal and a gilded wood-and-iron "Gustavian" chandelier from Dennis & Leen. Zuber "Paysage Italien" panels above each fireplace bring the garden indoors. Note the room-sized Oushak carpet from A.M.S. that anchors the room in purposefully muted tones.

mesh "Obelisk" pedestal was placed in the center as counterpoint to the room's formality, and a pair of Donghia "Shell" chairs upholstered in Clarence House's engaging zebra-striped "Swifty" were added beneath. Bespoke and repurposed accent pieces were chosen in juxtaposition to the room's grandeur, including a gold-leafed log stool from the Phillips Collection, a 1920s chinoiserie floor lamp, and a crusty iron French bistro table from Randall Tysinger.

A classic library was designed adjacent to the living room, its two stories of oak shelves capped by a frieze of favorite quotations carved around the top. An antique Oushak in fiery vermilion, brick, orange and gold generated the palette of the room; its warm tones were repeated in drapery panels of "Ravi," a printed linen paisley from Old World Weavers. A sofa from the owners' previous residence was updated with new upholstery in corresponding autumnal hues: copper "Monroe" from Watts of Westminster on the body, with back cushions of Quadrille "Pemberto Paisley" and kidney pillows of David Hicks' "Hexagon House Chenille," which was also used for a lounge chair from Hancock and Moore. An antique oak library table highlighted by a handsome skirt of Gothic tracery was placed in the window with a mid-nineteenth-century iron statue of Clio, the Muse of History, resting on top for an appropriately studious and meditative accent.

AN ELLIPTICAL bay at the end of the master bedroom lets light from the meditation garden spill into the room. Drapery panels of Hodsoll McKenzie "Indian Cartouche" in honey, topaz, celadon and beige add warmth and pattern along with a "Thicket" Tibetan wool rug from Odegard. The "Prince Charles" tester from Rose Tarlow is covered with Travers' duck egg blue "Pavilion" linen and accented with a mint-colored embroidered silk border from Scalamandré, *facing.*

SEATING IN FRONT of the fireplace includes a pair of Brunschwig and Fils "Beaumont" lounge chairs. An opaline glass lamp lights the celadon and gold leafed Niermann Weeks commode, set beneath a Rococo piecrust mirror from Panache.

The new master suite

was purposefully located on the first floor, beyond the library and easily accessible to the gardens as well as the main living areas of the home. The theme of neoclassic architecture was continued with a barrel-vaulted ceiling and a light-filled elliptical bay on the far end of the room, opening to a softly splashing fountain and meditation garden outside. Bespoke items included a pair of garden caryatids, given new life as pilas-

ters for the fireplace. A "Prince Charles" canopied tester bed from Rose Tarlow was given privacy with translucent horse hair-and-linen sheers. Matching Brunschwig & Fils "Beaumont" lounge chairs were set in front of the fireplace, upholstered in a vine-covered velvet from Jack L. Larsen, their golden tones accented by a pair of bow-front celadon and gold leaf–stenciled commodes from Niermann Weeks on either side.

HER MASTER BATH is an exotic escape with an antique Syrian mirror and a pair of etched chinoiserie mirrored wall lights from Vaughan over the marble commode. Venetian plaster walls in a pale celadon complement the fixtures.

H

is and hers studies, dressing rooms and baths were designed with convenience and comfort in mind. Her bath was given the exotic allure of the Far East with a Ming Dynasty wooden screen found on a trip to China suspended behind an eighteenth-century Carrara marble sarcophagus tub in the center of the room. The exotic beauty of the East is further emphasized with an antique Indian side chair inlaid with camel bone and mother-of-pearl next to the tub, and a similarly inlaid and carved Syrian mirror above the commode.

LINEN "SILVERTREE" toile draperies from Kathryn Ireland filter the morning sunlight behind a carved-teak Ming Dynasty screen suspended above the eighteenth-century sarcophagus tub. The stone mosaic floor is from Walker Zanger and all plumbing fixtures are from Waterworks.

THE OCTAGONAL
supper room opens off
the back hall and is used
for games and small
suppers. The paneled
walls are heavily glazed
over Farrow & Ball
"Calke Green," and the
windows and ceiling are
covered in a Jasper linen
print. An antique marble
garden statue, one of a
set of the Four Seasons,
gazes reflectively from a
niche across the room. A
crusty iron "Provencale"
chandelier from David
Iatesta hangs above the
antique Georgian table
in the center, *facing*.

THE BACK HALL
functions as an intimate
passageway from the
formal rooms to the
family living quarters.
Wall panels were inset
with Michael C. Smith's
"Indian Flower" linen;
the left wall panels
are cleverly designed
to conceal storage
closets behind. A trio
of pendant lights with
ivory paper shades is
from Object Insolite.
An antique, carved
stone eagle rests on a
metal mesh pedestal
as a focal point in the
niche beyond, *right*.

Informal family living quarters
were created in the new southern wing of the
house, accessed thru a passageway paneled
in rectangles of Michael C. Smith's Jasper
Collection "Indian Flower," a linen printed
in warm tones of honey, sienna, olive and
blue-green. An octagonal supper room was
added as an intimate space for games or
small suppers, its paneled walls glazed with
Farrow & Ball's deep "Calke Green." "Indian
Flower" was used again here for draperies as
well as the ceiling. The room was centered on
a circular Georgian period table with original
leather top, set with Hickory fruitwood chairs
upholstered with patterned leather seats and
Fortuny "Caravaggio" on their backs.

BARRY'S CERUSED oak "Michael" sofa lends an Arts and Crafts sensibility with iron joints and wooden pegging. A "Henley" rush-seated, walnut-stained oak armchair from Rose Tarlow and an antique walnut candle stand are warm wooden accents. Linen draperies are "Flying Ducks" from Mulberry Home.

The family room at the end of the passageway was created in the style of an English manor great hall, with paneled oak walls and a soaring beamed and vaulted Gothic ceiling. A pair of "Solana" sofas from R. Jones upholstered in chocolate velvet "Panzano" from S. Harris was set in front of the fireplace, along with two lounge chairs from Tomlinson that swivel on their bases. Mementos from travels around the world that give the room an eclectic and personal touch include woven baskets from Africa and clay jugs from Morocco on the mantel. Barry's cerused oak "Michael" sofa, covered in a persimmon and chocolate woven fabric from Lee Jofa, was nestled next to the broad window bay overlooking the rose gardens.

THE TWO-STORY vaulted family room is covered in oak paneling with a frieze of "Samoa," a woven herringbone-patterned straw matting from Newcastle Wallcoverings. A casual seating area in front of the fireplace is centered on a large ottoman from George Smith, covered with Watts of Westminster "Dore Lily" in rose truffle. Symmetry is emphasized with a pair of swivel lounge chairs from Tomlinson upholstered in Quadrille's woven bargello "Aladdin," two sofas from R. Jones covered in S. Harris "Panzano" linen, and a pair of Donghia "Zig Zag" floor lamps.

UPPER GLASS-PANED cabinets in the kitchen are painted in Farrow & Ball "String." Old World Weavers "Savita" crewel is continued from the morning room as a Roman shade to tie the adjacent spaces together.

A HIGH, barrel-vaulted ceiling lit by a glass dome lets light stream into the morning room and open kitchen (to the right). Cheerful citrus colors are emphasized with a yellow-to-orange ombred Panama straw rug below, its circular shape complemented by Barry's round "Dana" ottoman. Barry's "Orkney" chair is upholstered in "Judd Check," a bright vermilion plaid from Clarence House, and a "Temple Floor Lamp" from Jamie Young provides light.

Inspired by Sir John Soane's famous London home, the morning room, opening off the family room, is lit by a vaulted, glass-domed ceiling. Anchored by a circular Panama straw rug from Timothy Paul woven in an ombre of color from pumpkin to marigold and red-orange, the room is warm and sunny, a perfect place for breakfast or a quick lunch. Barry's "Orkney" chair was covered in "Judd Check," a bold vermilion plaid from Clarence House, as a bright and cheerful accent. Yellow, pimento and olive embroidery on the crewel patterned "Savita" curtains from Old World Weavers continue the sunny colors across the French doors and into the adjacent kitchen, where it was used as a Roman shade above the stone farmhouse sink. Honed granite counters and backsplash, a riveted steel hood by Kelly Metalworks above the range, and quarter-sawn oak cabinets give the kitchen an honest, Craftsman appeal.

INDOOR OUTDOOR fabrics selected to withstand water and sun includes Giati's lime green "Beachside Stripe" on a pair of teak lounges. Drapery panels of a China Seas printed linen in chocolate and lime provides a complementary accent. A concrete "Euphrates" cocktail table from Stoneyard centers the seating area in front of Barry's "Robertson" sofa, while an Avery Boardman sleeper sofa at the far end of the room, along with a kitchenette and bath on the opposite end, allows the space to double as a guesthouse when needed.

A new pool and pool house were designed for the rear gardens newly laid out by landscape gardener Ben Page. Walls of French glass doors that retract and disappear transform the space into an open-air pavilion surrounded by the gardens, while distressed board-and-batten walls and a cobbled slate floor lend a comfortable, timeworn patina. Complete with a small kitchen and large bath, the pool house can also accommodate overnight guests. Furnishings that wouldn't be damaged by moisture were selected, including a pair of Southerland "Louis Soleil" teak lounge chairs covered in lime green indoor-outdoor fabric and accented with Giati's "Corduroy Chocolate" in a vertical stripe. A pair of sofas—Barry's "Robertson," covered in Donghia's bisque "Krazy Quilt" matelassé, and a sleeper sofa from Avery Boardman, upholstered in "Melong Batik" from Quadrille's China Seas—provide large-scale comfortable seating.

Traditional yet functional for a modern family, this classic Southern home has been brought forward into the twenty-first century in a graceful and timeless manner.

Barry's **Tips**

Don't be afraid to mix metallic finishes—silver, copper, brass and gold—together for an elegant look. Better to mix than match.

Repurpose favorite furnishings with new upholstery and/or finishes for a sense of consistency.

Upholster the walls of a dining room to minimize noise and make dining more intimate.

Add a whimsical accent, such as a gilded tree-stump table, to prevent a formal room from becoming too serious and grand.

Favored mementos in an entry give visitors a personal sense of welcome.

Industrial Redux
IN CORINTH, MISSISSIPPI

BARRY WAS ASKED TO CONVERT A VACANT BRICK BUILDING DOWNTOWN INTO AN URBAN LOFT, A GETAWAY FOR WEEKENDS AND FAMILY RETREATS.

Corinth, Mississippi, is a small town in the rural South that time has passed by. While it escaped being burned by the North during the Civil War and its streets are still lined with gracious antebellum homes, the downtown has suffered the fate of many small towns across America. Many of its nineteenth-century brick storefronts lie vacant, and people now shop at the malls on the city's outskirts. Barry's client had been raised here and returned for frequent visits. Committed to

A SEATING AREA for morning coffee in the master bedroom has an antique walnut marble-topped table and a pair of Dessin Fournir side chairs upholstered in Yoma velvets with café-colored "Lyon" on the seats and inside backs, and misty-blue "Capri" on the outside backs. The master bath is glimpsed through the translucent rolling glass doors beyond, *facing*.

SLATE RISERS laid on a chevron pattern echo the floor in the first-floor entry. Walls are painted in Farrow & Ball "String," *left*.

BARRY KNEW THAT IT WAS IMPORTANT
TO REMAIN TRUE TO THE BUILDING'S INTEGRITY, AND THUS STRUCTURAL ELEMENTS WERE CELEBRATED AS THE BACKBONE OF THE RESTORATION.

revitalizing his hometown, he asked Barry to help start a trend and help him convert one of the vacant brick buildings downtown into an urban loft, a getaway for weekends and family retreats. Built in the 1860s, the space was admittedly in poor condition: boarded up, it hadn't seen daylight for decades, the ceilings were collapsing and the plaster was crumbling off the walls. But the location overlooking Main Street was ideal, and once the arched double-hung windows were uncovered, light poured inside.

Originally an area for grain storage for the general store downstairs, the second floor was modest and had never been a residential structure. Working closely with New Orleans architect Dennis Brady, Barry began with the basics: new stairs and an elevator were added for convenient access, and the interior spaces were opened to light with the addition of rooftop skylights. He knew that it was important to remain true to the building's integrity, and thus structural elements were celebrated as the backbone of the restoration. Rather than add new drywall and plaster throughout, the original brick

walls were preserved, lightly sandblasted and then simply sealed with four layers of a matte sealer to protect their original patina and character. Elements were kept open and honest: conduits and pipes were left exposed, wooden ceilings were salvaged or, when necessary, replaced with repurposed heart pine, and even old graffiti was deliberately left intact as a romantic link to the building's nineteenth-century original occupants and generations since. To help make the loft seem larger, the main living areas—living room, dining room and kitchen—were kept open and fluid, defined simply by movable translucent horsehair-and-linen sheers hung on iron rods suspended from the ceiling.

Space was reconfigured with the addition of two bedrooms, two and one-half baths, and much-needed storage. Indigenous materials were chosen to complement and blend seamlessly with the originals—exposed copper tubing to highlight the terra-cotta red of the reclaimed, locally fired brick, gunmetal gray finishes on vanities and commodes to echo the building's industrial past, and oil-rubbed bronze Baxter hardware for vintage appeal.

A "BRANWEN" natural iron bed from Ironies is complemented by a treelike metal bedside table. The rich tones of the deconstructed plaster and brick walls are softened by fabrics, including the olive, plum and silvery gold of Fortuny's "Canestrelli" pillow. The swing-arm wall sconce is by David Easton, *facing*.

A CUSTOM CONSOLE in the master bath was kept simple and honest with exposed copper pipes and a stainless steel structure. Organic elements were reinforced with a columnar stone lamp from Robert Abbey. Farrow & Ball's watery blue "Borrowed Light" on the walls is reflected in the shagreen and nickel-studded wall mirror above, from Avery Fine Art, *right*.

WATERWORKS' "Bateau" soaking tub reflects the soft taupe and gray tones of the mosaic floor. "Granada" draperies from Tyler Graphics through Timothy Paul were continued from the master bedroom, *right below*.

A master suite was created at the back of the apartment, the salvaged charcoal-colored brick and plaster walls providing the backbone for the room's palette and design. A bed from Ironies was selected to center the space; its headboard was upholstered in café-colored "Lyon" velvet from Yoma and the canopy was hung with Tyler Graphics "Granada," whose hand-blocked linen in celadon, taupe and duck-egg blue was a soft and pleasing contrast to the deconstructed surroundings. A comfortable sitting area was arranged in front of the windows, centered on an antique marble-topped table set with a pair of walnut "Lambert" side chairs from Dessin Fournir and Barry's inviting "Middleburg" chaise, upholstered in a textured linen from Kathryn Ireland.

Sandblasted rolling glass doors were installed as a translucent screen for the adjacent master bath. Exposed brick walls, a mosaic slate floor in rich hues of taupe and smoky gray, and a custom vanity constructed from bars of stainless steel with a honed stone top were combined for an industrial overture.

THE FOB on Barry's "Middleburg" chaise references horse hitching posts on Corinth's Main Street a century ago, *below*.

Gothic arched windows

at the front of the loft were used as the outline for a pair of twin headboards in the guest bedroom. Their shapes were accented with flat "Warwick" picot braid trim from Samuel & Sons in a natural burlap color and highlighted with a border of decorative nail heads finished in gunmetal gray. The walls were carefully sealed and preserved, including nineteenth-century weight measurements still visible on the old plaster. A pair of simple wooden "Ceres" chairs from Ironies, a woolen rug from Floor Gallery in soothing sea foam green, and a goatskin-covered bench from Oly kept the room unassuming yet still inviting, a comfortable retreat for weekend visitors.

HEADBOARDS FOR the twin beds were based on arched Gothic windows at the front of the loft. A "Breton" cast brass and shagreen side table by Ironies rests in between, while a skylight provides additional light, *above*.

MARKS & MEASUREMENTS on the original plaster walls were carefully preserved as romantic links to the loft's past. Yoma's duck egg blue "Mockingbird" suede covers the Gothic headboard and bed and is accented with a pillow of "Donuts," a lively Galbraith & Paul hand-painted linen. The seat of Ironies' "Ceres" chair is upholstered in Pollack's linen "Knitwork" in neutral "Stream," *facing*.

A

clerestory ceiling was in-
stalled to allow natural light to penetrate the
interior of the loft over the centrally located
kitchen and adjacent family room. The look
of a vintage laboratory was created in the
kitchen, with sandblasted glass cabinets by
SieMatic contrasted against walls of dark-
ened, acid-etched steel. A pair of distressed
wood bar chairs stand at the counter under
a trio of brushed steel pendant "Astrid"
lights from Ironware International. A family reading area was created just beyond
the kitchen. An antique oak Morris chair,
still with its original honey-colored leather
seat cushion, and a pair of Barry's wingback "Shawn" chairs loosely upholstered in
Clarence House's cocoa-colored "Luchino"
linen were grouped around a lotus-shaped
willow hassock from Palecek that was covered in pear-green cotton velvet. Architectural salvage was used to anchor the area—
a glass-front cabinet constructed from old
wavy glass windows set against the wall, its
worn and partially stripped wooden window
frames and vintage brass hardware deliberately left intact and imperfect.

"CLOUSEAUX" plantation-style dining chairs from Hickory Chair are an appropriate complement to the loft's nineteenth-century sienna and ecru-colored plaster and brick walls *below*.

Movable translucent

sheers suspended from iron ceiling rods define the dining room alcove in the center of the loft. A strikingly elliptical "Alessio" dining table set on a base of intersecting Xs anchors the area and is lit by a low-hanging circular "Harness" chandelier by Kevin Reilly from Holly Hunt, its iron construction referencing the iron ceiling rods above. Plantation-style cane-back "Clouseaux" dining chairs from Hickory Chair were selected to allow air and light circulation for diners seated at the table, a thoughtful courtesy for those often warm Southern evenings.

THE DINING ALCOVE is defined by movable, translucent "Camarague" horsehair-and-linen sheers from Timothy Paul. The elliptical shape of Formations' "Alessio" dining table is echoed by the grand piano in the living room beyond. The seats of the dining chairs were covered in Clarence House's taupe and gold "Messina," *above*.

A NINETEENTH-CENTURY Italian walnut and marble-topped console from a Southern estate anchors the far wall of the dining alcove. Note that the wiring conduits were deliberately left exposed, emphasizing the industrial character of the restoration, *facing*.

LIGHT SOFTLY
filters into a corner of
the living room through
drapery panels of silk and
cotton "Rose de Roi" from
Tyler Graphics. Pillows
in Fortuny's rich green
and gold "Richelieu"
provide an elegant
accent. A flat-weave
wool rug in woodland
tones of mahogany,
walnut and soft grays
from AMS Rugs ties the
room together, *facing*.

**AN EIGHTEENTH-
CENTURY** Corinthian
column with original
finish was made into
a floor lamp, *right*.

The living room at the front of the loft was divided into areas for music and conversation, with an ebonized grand piano anchoring one end of the room. Furnishings were kept comfortable and eclectic, as if they had been gathered from family homes over time: a vintage Chesterfield leather sofa updated with cushions in Clarence House's organic "Kasuma" tapestry, a pair of ebonized bobbin chairs from Formations, Barry's "Robertson" day bench in cerused oak upholstered in Myung Jin's stone-colored "Swirl." Softly draped panels of Tyler Graphic's hand-block-printed cotton-and-silk "Rose de Roi" in soft russet, olive and coffee browns were hung at the windows, their muted tones forming the perfect complement to the earthen and bronze hues of the loft's salvaged plaster and brick walls. A mica-encrusted pier mirror from Niermann Weeks was hung on the wall to enlarge the space; its sparkling, beveled glass gave additional depth and dimension.

With respect for the building's origins and the skillful juxtaposition of materials both old and new, this once-abandoned loft has been given a new lease on life. Its restoration turned out to be quite a success, stimulating similar projects and development on Main Street, bringing life and vitality back to Corinth's downtown core—precisely what the owner had hoped for.

A PASTICHE of time and ornament defines the living room at the front of the loft. A Syrian bench covered in sparkling mother-of-pearl rests against the far wall. Dessin Fournir's "Lexington" club chair and matching ottoman upholstered in Old World Weavers' beige "Turis" is angled toward the view over Main Street.

Barry's Tips

Hang a painting in front of a scrim or curtain to define a space and create an instant gallery.

Update a tired leather sofa by re-upholstering its seat cushions in a graphic, modern fabric.

Choose reclaimed wood not only for its beauty but to be eco-friendly: it is carbon neutral and preserves the environment.

Take out a hall closet and create a niche for reading or working on the computer.

Celebrate a building's origins—preserve old brick and plaster by cleaning and applying a matte sealer.

Modern Living
IN AN HISTORIC ROWHOUSE ON CAPITOL HILL

THE TRANSFORMATION IN THE NARROW HOME WAS DRAMATIC. FAMILY FURNISHINGS WERE GIVEN NEW LIFE WITH STYLE AND SOPHISTICATION.

The owners, a young couple with one toddler and another on the way, contacted Barry with a unique set of needs. They owned a Victorian rowhouse on Washington DC's historic Capitol Hill and were committed to the neighborhood, with its handsome brick homes, culturally diverse markets and proximity to the Capitol. But they needed a contemporary and functional living space, a home for a growing family that could withstand curious hands and little fingers, with furnishings that were durable

THE FOYER WAS LIGHTENED WITH FARROW & BALL "CLUNCH" FOR CRISP, CONTEMPORARY APPEAL. FLOORS THROUGHOUT THE HOME WERE REFINISHED AND STAINED A LUSTROUS ESPRESSO BROWN, AND DETAILS SUCH AS THE HANDSOMELY TURNED BALUSTRADES WERE BRIGHTENED.

and easy to clean but still had style and sophistication.

They worked closely with architect Evan Lippencott, who was well versed in local building codes and restrictions, as all exterior changes needed to pass Capitol Hill's strict architectural review board. As the house and lot were narrow and deep, a three-story rear extension was designed to expand it unobtrusively, adding a bright and sunny family kitchen and living area on the main floor, with office and guest suites on the lower level and bedroom space upstairs. Rooms throughout the home were streamlined, while original detailing such as pocket doors and handsome molding was carefully preserved. A major interior change was to open the dark central staircase to light and circulation by removing the adjacent wall to the dining room, replacing it with a large cased opening flanked by a pair of clas-

sic fluted columns. The transformation in the narrow home was dramatic: light now flooded into the staircase from the dining room windows, allowing the stairwell to become a vertical art gallery and, in addition, giving six more feet of visual space in the dining room.

The foyer was lightened with Farrow & Ball "Clunch" for crisp, contemporary appeal. Floors throughout the home were refinished and stained a lustrous espresso brown, and details such as the handsomely turned balustrades were brightened. Family furnishings were given new life: a vintage brown settee was lacquered in creamy white and its faded tapestry upholstery was replaced with a dynamic espresso, fuchsia and tangerine woven. An overscale mirror with a lemon gilt finish opened the small foyer to reflected light and helped diminish its angularity.

A VIBRANT WATERCOLOR from Natural Curiosities rests above the fireplace and is complemented by organic accents—tree lichen, coral dahlias from the garden, and twigs in the fireplace below, *facing*.

A STREAMLINED and child-friendly sofa from Stewart fits nicely in the bay, and the room is centered on a cheerful pink ottoman. A throw pillow in Schumacher "Reflex," in waves of hot pink, raspberry and chocolate, adds a burst of color. Simple Henry Calvin "Brussels" gauze sheers are an economical window treatment, trimmed here with a coral Greek key banding from Samuel & Sons.

he living room was given color and interest for the young family, with cheerful pinks and greens played against rich browns and crisp whites. Furniture was placed around a round ottoman covered in Valtekz's shell-pink shagreen by Celerie Kemble. A pair of French club chairs from Niermann Weeks, covered in Barry's woven "Crop Art Circles" for Vervain, orbit the ottoman, while a mirrored ceiling medallion surrounding a bell jar lantern from Chameleon anchors the vortex above. A clean-line, low-profile sofa from Stewart was placed in the front bay, upholstered in Schumacher "Shake It Up," a cream-colored woven. Window coverings were deliberately kept simple and economical with gauzy sheers. The original mantelpiece was freshened with Farrow & Ball "Clunch" (used on the walls as well), and a note of luxury and warmth was introduced with intimate side niches upholstered in Bergamo's silk damask "Edo" in cocoa brown.

A TRIPTYCH of a horse by Christopher Wilcox draws the eye into the stairwell gallery.

A JIB DOOR with studies of floor tiles in acrylic frames from Natural Curiosities hung down its length accesses the pantry and kitchen. A deconstructed finish on the base of the concrete dining table and a cast-stone top from Ironies are relaxed and modern accents.

ocket doors leading into the adjoining dining room were conserved, and the room was substantially enlarged by the removal of the wall into the central hall. Inspired by the columns flanking the fireplace, a pair of large fluted columns capped with Ionic capitals was added for a sense of architectural cohesiveness. Family-friendly furnishings included a deconstructed concrete-base dining table with a dark, cast-stone top from Ironies and Zentique's Louis XVI–style chairs upholstered in a natural cocoa-colored linen. Two custom curved macassar ebony–veneered storage cabinets from Mitchell Yanosky were added for much-needed storage.

The family kitchen and open living space beyond occupies the new rear addition. Sunny and happy tones of kiwi and orange were mixed with chocolate for a color scheme the children would enjoy. A central cooking and food prep island doubles as a breakfast bar.

A

coffered ceiling unifying the kitchen and living areas was painted with Ralph Lauren "Buckskin Suede" for a textured contrast. Cheerful curtains in persimmon, chocolate and apple green add a bold organic note. Furnishings were kept child-friendly with low seating and rounded edges—round bronze coffee and side tables from Oly, Barry's "Robertson" sofa upholstered in Donghia "Krazy Quilt" cotton matelassé, and a pair of "Thompson" side chairs from Hickory Chairs.

A COZY CORNER for breakfast is set with a Saarinen table from Knole and Designer Workshops' bentwood chairs, *far left*.

THE CHEERFUL palette of tangerine and olive carries through from the living room to the open kitchen. SieMatic translucent glass cabinets float on a shimmering wall of penny-dot glass tiles from Waterworks. Amber glass pendant lights from Jamie Young illuminate the center island.

THE IRIDESCENT silver and gray palette continues in the master bath, which boasts a deep soaking tub. Pale celadon and jade green river stone floors are a pleasing complement to the glimmering surfaces, *above left*.

AN "ETOILE" double lavatory from Waterworks, lit by Murano glass sconces, is seen through the freestanding glass-enclosed shower across the room, *below left*.

"FELICIA," a ripple-fold natural linen from Chris Stono, is used for drapery panels in the master bedroom. Note how the drapery tracks are set into the ceiling for maximum height. A matelassé woven coverlet from Ankasa covers the bed, which is flanked by library shelves on either side, *right*.

While the owners wanted a library, space was at a premium, so a curtained wall of books was created behind the low upholstered headboard of the "Sonoma" bed from Stewart in the master suite. Walls were painted with Ralph Lauren "Regent Metallic," a reflective pewter, for an elegant urban appeal but without the cost of silvered wallpaper. "Felicia," a toast-colored linen from Chris Stone, was used for draperies on the windows as a subtle complement and repeated in the panels across the bookshelves. The sleek silvery palette was continued in the adjoining master bath, accented with a nickel-plated tea table from Four Hands and a smoke bell lantern from Baker overhead.

OVERSCALE ARTWORK brightens the hallway to the boys' bedrooms. Simple linen draperies from Pottery Barn are a low-cost solution, with walls painted Farrow & Ball "Sky Blue" for a serene yet colorful note, *below*.

The boys' rooms were kept bright and elemental, easy to update as required. Furnishings were simple—an inherited bed and a nightstand that doubles as a handy spot for toy storage. Walls were painted Farrow & Ball's calming "Sky Blue," a soothing color for naptime.

Tailored and sophisticated, the Victorian townhouse has been reinterpreted. Brought forward for a young family of the twenty-first century, it has been updated with an engaging color palette and furnishings to please both young children and adults alike.

THE BOYS' SHARED bath is completely tiled in creamy subway tiles from Waterworks for easy maintenance. Round mirrors above the Kohler sinks reference airplane portholes in the print on the wall, *above*.

A FAMILY BED is updated with John Robshaw's cocoa and white "Star Quilt" comforter and "Gent's Stripe" dust skirt underneath. The simple night table also provides storage for toys, *facing*.

Barry's **Tips**

Use a palette with bright accents of color to stimulate both children and adults.

If you have toddlers, employ low seating with rounded edges and soft corners for their convenience and safety.

Introduce drama and sheen into a room with metallic paints at a fraction of the cost of reflective wallpapers.

If space is limited, put a library in the bedroom, dining room or hall and screen the shelves with curtains.

Try a mirrored ceiling medallion to subtly reflect light and create a sparkling focus overhead.

Georgian Tradition
ON THE POTOMAC

VALUES OF SYMMETRY, BALANCE, & PROPORTION IN A HOME FIRMLY CONNECTED TO THE PROPERTY WITH VIEWS OF THE RIVER.

Potomac, Maryland, hasn't changed much over time. It is a sylvan retreat of gracious homes set amongst woodlands just outside the hustle and bustle of metropolitan Washington, D.C. The homeowner was raised here and loves its peaceful setting on the banks of the Potomac River. But the family house was modestly scaled and no longer met the needs of their large extended family. Working with architect Geri Yantis, Barry designed a completely new residence, one that was inspired

THE OWNER'S ANTIQUE MAJOLICA inspired the colors and patterns of the garden room's fabrics: quilted chartreuse leaf-like matelassé from Donghia on the Odalisque sofa, and a graphic floral and vine print from Oscar de la Renta on the accent pillows, *right*.

CHISELED BEAUMANIERE limestone imported from France gives the entrance hall and garden room beyond the cool sophistication of a European country house. A pair of nineteenth-century carved oak chairs with their original butternut yellow leather upholstery, a Georgian soft green leather wing chair, and an eighteenth-century tea table complement the stone-colored Venetian plaster walls. A classic pedimented archway frames the light filled garden room beyond, which is anchored by Barry's "Odalisque" sofa for Tomlinson/ Erwin-Lambeth, *facing*.

RECLAIMED HEART PINE WAS FOUND FOR FLOORS AND PANELING, ALONG WITH BEAUMANIERE LIMESTONE, WHICH WAS LAID IN THE STAIRWELL.

by traditional Georgian architecture and its values of symmetry, balance, and proportion, a home firmly connected to the property with views of the river and the surrounding landscape that could accommodate children, grandchildren, and guests in an elegant and inviting manner.

The first year was spent planning so that the project would go smoothly and remain on schedule; every detail was reviewed and furnishings were ordered well in advance, ensuring the home would be ready to move into as soon as construction was complete. Rooms were designed with good bones and the best of classic Georgian proportion and symmetry. Venetian plaster walls were highlighted with hand-cast plaster cor-

nices, dentil work, and trim; twelve-foot ceilings were supported by classic pilasters capped with decorative capitals; and ornate entablatures were created above many of the doorways. Reclaimed heart pine was found for floors and paneling, along with Beaumaniere limestone, which was laid in the stairwell and garden room, lending age and patina. A classically proportionate entry hall with a bowed plaster ceiling and honeycombed parquetry floor in walnut, oak, and pear wood, was created to welcome visitors inside. Its walls were painted in Farrow & Ball's country house "Calke Green" (based on the color found in the baroque eighteenth-century Calke Abbey in England).

THE SERIOUSNESS OF AN ANTIQUE Italian console is relieved with a table lamp made from a simple terra-cotta balustrade, *facing*. An eighteenth-century gilded Italian console gleams against Scalamandré's damask drapes, *facing*.

THE MATTE WOODEN TOGGLE TRIM from Samuel & Sons is played against the dresser finishes, *right*.

A

pair of parlors was designed on either side of the entry hall—to the right, an intimate and elegant formal room for small gatherings before or after dinner. Its walls and windows were enveloped in Scalamandré's chocolate brown silk damask "Gabrielle," the rich dark tones set against the gleam of a pair of gilded eighteenth-century carved Italian consoles in front of the windows. A deeply recessed coffered ceiling was created for intimacy and the room was comfortably furnished with a pair of curved O. Henry House sofas with a Rose Tarlow ebony veneered "O'Kelly" table, delicately painted with flowers and vines, in between. A pair of glass-paned built-in cabinets was added on either side of the door to display the owner's collection of antique Wedgwood ceramics, whose classic urn motif was repeated in plaster friezes on the cornice. Salvaged terra-cotta balustrades from a nineteenth-century garden pavilion were made into a pair of lamps and placed on the gilded consoles, counterpoints to the room's formality.

FRENCH DOORS lead from the entry foyer into the formal parlor, *above left*.

A DETAIL OF THE VALANCE in the formal parlor shows the attention to detail—note how the pattern of the Scalamandré damask is complemented by the plaster molding above, *left*.

THE FORMAL FRONT
PARLOR is a chocolate
confection with Scalamandré's
rich brown silk damask
"Gabrielle" used for the window
treatments as well as upholstery
on the walls. Bergamo's "Prisca

Germoglio" soft green silk pillows
soften the curved backs of a pair
of curved O. Henry House sofas
in the center of the room. The
coffered honeycombed ceiling
adds an opulent note, *above*.

THE LIVING ROOM is sunny and cheerful in colors of melon, vermilion, and soft garden greens. Note the use of rugs to define conversation areas—a round sea grass carpet from Floor Gallery edged with Bergamo "La Fontaine" melon velvet to anchor the Rose Tarlow table and Barry's "Barrymore" chaise in the foreground, and an antique Turkish Oushak to center the settee in the window, *left*.

CLASSIC ORNAMENT helps define the living room entrance and relate it to the entry hall and formal parlor beyond. Walls are painted in Farrow & Ball "Fowler Pink," a calming backdrop to the summery palette. Hues in similar tones were used to coordinate and balance the room: Quadrille's leafy vermilion silk "Flamingo Flame" upholsters a pair of Donghia "Shell" chairs, and "Aveley," a salmon-colored textured chenille from Zoffany, is on the settee. Celadon green pillows from Fortuny on the sofa provide a pleasing contrast, *right*.

To the left of the entry hall, a warm and open living room was created in organic colors of melon, tangerine, and celery; the walls were painted Farrow & Ball's light terra-cotta "Fowler Pink." Accented with hand-cast entablatures above the doors and recessed niches on either side that hold a pair of large nine-teenth-century garden urns, the room beckons with the lightness and charm of an English country garden. A pair of softly curved Donghia "Shell" chairs upholstered in Quadrille's leafy vermil-ion silk "Flamingo Flame" flank a Dennis & Leen settee covered in "Aveley," a salmon-colored textured chenille from

Zoffany, adding to the room's bright and flowery palette. Across the room, Barry's "Barrymore" chaise is nestled next to Rose Tarlow's "Gladstone" lounge chair, with dragonflies flitting across its Clarence House peachy velvet. As the room was large, conversation areas were defined by a combination of smaller carpets—an antique Turkish Oushak rug in soft green and salmon in front of the settee, and a round carpet of neutral sea grass bordered with melon velvet to anchor the furnishings in the center of the room. Bennison's cheerful "Tree Flower" floral linen curtains flank each window as catalysts for the room's varied tones.

REPETITION OF MOTIFS on the dining room mantel subtly strengthens the room's overall design: the carved urn is reflected in a silver tureen above, while a painted dove is repeated in the surrounding Gracie wall covering.

The owners love to entertain friends and family (Thanksgiving dinners traditionally serve scores of guests) and a spacious dining room was a must. Subtly layering floral motifs in the thirty-foot-long room, Barry began with hand-painted Gracie wallpaper panels of blossoms and birds in soft hues of moss green, stone, and parchment, enveloping it in a leafy bower. The canopy was anchored with a custom-designed hooked rug from Elizabeth Eakins in an organic Arts and Crafts floral pattern underneath.

IN THE DINING ROOM, Barry's "Albemarle" chairs are covered in an organically textured fabric from Quadrille. Antiques anchor the end of the room, including an eighteenth-century mahogany buffet and ornately hard-carved and water-gilded looking glass from the 1840s. A silver punch bowl holds a mound of fresh flowers.

Barry's open-loop-back "Albemarle" chairs were set around the oval walnut and pear wood dining table for an effect of garden fretwork, while Fortuny's celery green "Granada" panels, dressed with goblet-pleated valances, were hung at the French doors, softening the space. Ornamental plasterwork continued the theme above with coved borders of acanthus leaves and olive branches cast to surround a central oval of fruits and vegetables: ears of corn, peas, berries, apples, and pears. A pair of chinoiserie-style lanterns from Niermann Weeks was hung above the dining table, much like exotic birdcages from Brighton Pavilion.

LIGHT FLOODS into the dining room through French doors that open to the terrace and rose gardens. Billowing panels of Fortuny's silvery-gold "Granada" help soften the space. Note the jib door leading to the butler's pantry beyond, *above.*

CUSTOM ORNAMENTAL plasterwork highlights the dining room ceiling with classical motifs, including fruits and vegetables, all by Jeff Schardt at Ornamental Plasterworks, *above right*.

FORTUNY'S "GRANADA" panels are accented with goblet pleats and gold Scalamandré bellflower trim. Simple wrought-iron rods soften the formality, *right*.

PORTIERES DIVIDING the kitchen from the family room are lined with the Chelsea Editions crewel fabric that was also used on the latter's windows. The multitasking center island has a stone top on one end for pastry, as well as a mesquite wooden top on the other end for dining, *facing*.

A JIB DOOR in the dining room opens into the pantry and is camouflaged by the carefully matched wallpaper. Details do make a difference—note how the sconce above the fireplace is hung in line with the pilaster, *right*.

A butler's pantry, cleverly camouflaged with a jib door covered with the Gracie panels (applied so the pattern was continuous when the door was either open or shut), connects to the kitchen beyond. Overlooking the rear terraces and gardens, a warm and inviting room was created with the help of Portfolio Kitchens. Anchored by a substantial hammered-bronze hood above the stove, set off by organic stone surrounds, the room is rustic yet functional and up-to-date. A multipurpose island in the kitchen's center was designed for both food prep (with a stone countertop on one end) and informal dining (with a mesquite wooden surface). Walls were papered in Morris "Rabbit" in a warm stone colorway, and the Arts and Crafts atmosphere was accented with a combination of antiques and comfortable furnishings—a vintage washed-pine gateleg table, corner cabinets displaying the owner's collection of antique Majolica plates, and comfortable armchairs from Formations. Double-sided portieres hung between the kitchen and adjoining family room not only soften the room but conveniently close it off after dining (when dishes have yet to be done).

THE FAMILY ROOM is paneled in warm, honey-toned, reclaimed heart pine, which is relieved by the espresso-colored cast-concrete bolection mantel by Concrete Jungle and Dennis & Leen's gateleg walnut table (deepened with a green wash for more visual interest and depth). The arch of the Palladian windows and the curve of the table help relieve the linearity of the wall and ceiling grids, *facing*.

THE FAMILY ROOM PANELING slides open on a hidden track to reveal a large bar. The striped woven linen from Bergamo railroaded onto the Rose Tarlow chairs underscores the linearity of the woodwork. The agrarian painting is attributed to the nineteenth-century French painter Rosa Bonheur.

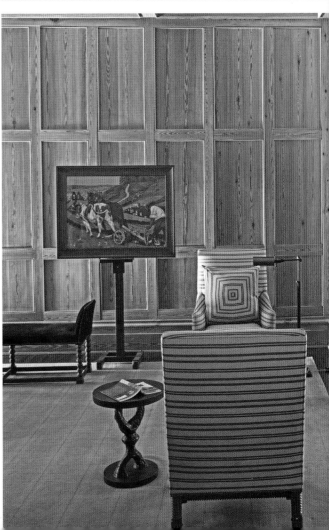

The family room was paneled in reclaimed heart pine, the panels being set on a hidden track to conceal a bar and storage area behind. The wood's warm honey tones were accented with a custom reversible cotton carpet from Elizabeth Eakins, woven in stripes of marigold and puce. Geometric pattern was further reinforced with a pair of Rose Tarlow chairs upholstered in a railroaded heavy-gauge woven linen stripe in flax, forest green, and cognac. An agrarian painting attributed to French painter Rosa Bonheur was highlighted on an easel, helping define the conversation area and separate it from the bar.

THE FAMILY ROOM is warm and welcoming as light pours in through French doors that open to the front terrace. Chelsea Edition's "Oak Leaves" in vine green filter the light. The arch of the Palladian windows helps relieve the linearity of the wall and ceiling grids.

THE MASTER SUITE
begins in the inviting sitting room, with Barry's curved "Maria" sofa nestled in the corner. A color palette of cool neutrals makes it a serene and restful space: Farrow & Ball "Old White" covers the woodwork and Sanderson "Sorilla" linen upholsters both the walls and the sofa. Additional seating includes an antique shield-back chair from Randall Tysinger Antiques and a pair of comfortably upholstered chairs from Dennis & Leen, *facing.*

A ROSE TARLOW hand-painted "Chang Console" side table holds a vintage '40s Lucite purse filled with flowers from the garden; the floral motif repeats in the bed hangings as well as in the Samuel & Sons "Harwick" cream embroidered ribbon trim on the bed pillows. The coverlet and bolsters are made of an informal "Krazy Quilt" cotton matelassé from Donghia in pale gray-green celadon and are lavishly trimmed with a hand-beaded galloon from Samuel and Sons, *right.*

Upstairs, a separate master suite allows the owners to relax in privacy. An inviting sitting room serves as the entrance; the room is crisp and inviting with Sanderson "Sorilla" linen in soft grays, greens, taupes, and beiges used on both the walls and the curved "Maria" sofa that Barry designed. A round wool "Vestry" Stark rug acts as a roundabout leading to the adjoining rooms—his-and-hers dressing areas, the master bedroom, and the outer hall. A gilt bronze and etched glass Vaughan lantern above a Dessin Fournir "Osterly" table centers the space, while a curved bookcase from Dennis & Leen adds height and presence to the corner.

Directly beyond the sitting room, the spacious master suite occupies the northeast corner of the home, its six windows affording views of the surrounding gardens.

THE MASTER BEDROOM'S ceiling is highlighted by classic ornamental plasterwork by Jeff Schardt, for the look of an English country house, and the room is anchored by a canopied Louis XVI mirrored bed from Julia Gray. Note the subtle but effective coordination of floral patterns, with Sanderson's larger scale "Borocay" used on the outer bed hangings that are lined with Sanderson's smaller-scaled, faded floral "Sorilla" linen on the interior bed curtains. Barry's "Barrymore" chair on the right is loosely upholstered in Boussac "Nandou."

The room, with its walls painted in Farrow & Ball's soothing "Celadon Green" and its ceiling accented with handsome custom plasterwork, welcomes with the ambience of an English country manor. A Louis XVI mirrored bed from Julia Gray sparkles and draws light into the center of the space, the reflection diffused with Sanderson's "Borocay" bed hangings lined with Sanderson's small floral linen "Sorilla" on the interiors. "Borocay" is repeated in the draperies at the windows to coordinate the pattern throughout the room. A separate sitting area in front of the fireplace is anchored by a pair of comfortably curved sofas from Niermann Weeks, while a wall-to-wall Lacy Champion wool carpet in a crisp linen white softens the floor underneath.

SANDERSON'S PALE celadon "Borocay" wallpaper in her bath complements the "Sorilla" floral cotton used for both the draw-back draperies and the vanity skirt. A jade green ceramic garden seat accents the room's garden tones. The 1930s Lucite English chair is an unexpected accent, *facing*.

A NICHE IN HIS MASTER BATH next to the stone fireplace holds an inherited antique mahogany chest-on-chest. Sanderson's "Borocay" draperies help soften the stone and tile surfaces, *right*.

ANTIQUE TRANSFERWARE rests on a "Baltic" vanity from Niermann Weeks in her bath, *below*.

The Sanderson linen draperies were continued in the wife's bath, where they were used on the windows as well as for a box-pleated skirt around the vanity. Octagons of cool limestone on the floor were randomly interspersed with sparkling art glass and carried up the wall to the windowsills, creating a visual illusion that heightened the windows, making them seem as if they still rested on the floor. A strikingly modern Lucite English armchair from the 1930s became a focal point of the bath, its original zebra-skin seat echoed in a zebra rug on the floor.

HIS MASTER BATH
is centered with a
burled walnut island to
make packing simple.
Walnut columns from
Ruth Livingston Studio
revolve to open, providing
storage for towels and
bath necessities. Note the
tumbled marble and slag
glass tile floor is carried up
to the windowsills to make
the room more intimate.
A floating vanity in front
of the window is wired
through hollow legs to hide
electric cords, *facing*.

The husband's master
bath and dressing room were designed with
every convenience in mind, from an island
set in the center of the room to simplify packing to a welcoming fireplace for those cold
and stormy winter evenings. The adjoining
dressing room is the ultimate in storage, an
arched classic enfilade of ten burled walnut
columns interspersed with book-matched
walnut closets and drawers.

IN HIS MASTER BATH
an enfilade of burled walnut
columns is interspersed
with closets and cabinets.
A natural wool runner from
Timothy Paul relieves
the rich tones of the
woodwork. The lanterns
are from the Baker Lighting
Collection, *above*.

THE GUEST BEDROOM'S furnishings are kept light with an open-legged Julia Gray sofa upholstered with Peter Fasano "Brompton" fabric and Hickory Chair's "Hedy" chair with "Skukusa" printed cotton from Sister Parish.

A  series of guest suites was added on the other end of the second floor, each providing a private retreat with an en suite bath. A trio of rooms was designed as an interior apartment, with two bedrooms joined by a sitting room in between, for their daughter, son-in-law, and their two young daughters. As the rooms overlook the rose gardens, the vermilion rose and moss greens of the view outdoors inspired the palette in the rooms. Cowtan & Tout "New Chantilly" floral linen was used to upholster the walls in the first bedroom and was pleasantly complemented by Osborne & Little's deep coral "Liberty Audsley" wallpaper in the sitting room and bedroom beyond tying the rooms together.

A GUEST BEDROOM is kept light and airy, its walls painted in Farrow & Ball "Estate Emulsion," with pale blue "Skylight' on the ceiling. A classic Lewis Mittman bed upholstered in Raoul Textile's "Sari Cardamon" printed linen is accented with a soft valance above in "Jacobean," Vervain's blue-green linen. Julia Gray mirrored cabinets on either side of the bed reflect light and space.

CREAMY WHITE
ranunculus fill this cornucopia porcelain vase under sconces from Marvin Alexander and are the perfect complement to the soft floral wall upholstery, *below*.

Soft valances over the windows echoed those over the beds and their silhouettes inspired the headboard. More garden-inspired colors were added with Merida's fresh "Living Coral" sisal carpet from Floor Gallery.

Color was the inspiration as well for another guest suite across the hall, whose walls were painted in Farrow & Ball "Estate Emulsion," with "Skylight" on the ceiling. Caribbean greens and aqua blues were continued with Vervain "Jacobean" linen used on both the windows and the valance above the Lewis Mittman bed, whose walnut frame is upholstered in "Sari Cardamon," a printed linen from Raoul Textiles.

Order and symmetry balanced with the best of classic design give this home a timeless elegance and appeal, making it not only a welcoming retreat for the current owners but a legacy they are proud to pass along to future generations.

THE SHAPE OF THE
window valances is echoed in the silhouette of the headboard, helping to tie the room's elements together. A cheerful orange lamp from Robert Abbey on the Niermann Weeks hand-painted nightstand adds a contemporary splash of color to the otherwise traditional room. The headboard and inner bed hangings are upholstered in Kathryn Ireland's "Papoose" in French gray and tomato, *above*.

REPETITION OF
pattern and color makes two bedrooms with a sitting room in between a separate suite. "New Chantilly" floral linen from Cowtan & Tout makes beautiful draperies and bed hangings, as well as wall upholstery, in the first bedroom. A Georgian rosewood desk from Randall Tysinger Antiques complements the reclaimed heart pine floors, *facing*.

EACH GRANDDAUGHTER gets her own twin bed accented with a glamorous printed linen canopy. Note the hand-worked accent pillows from John Robshaw, *facing*. BUILT-IN BOOKCASES provide touches of color and a library for guests on the upper mezzanine, *above*.

Barry's Tips

Everyday objects can be recycled as attention-getting containers for floral arrangements. Try a silver punch bowl, a creamer, or even an acrylic '40s pocketbook.

Use an architectural antique to loosen up a traditional setting, i.e., terra-cotta balustrades made into lamps help relax an otherwise formal parlor.

Reclaimed wood helps to make a home environmentally friendly and "green" as well as to lend it instant age and patina.

Rather than doors, portieres can screen a kitchen.

Run floor tile up to the windowsills in a high-ceilinged bath to make the windows seem taller and the room more intimate.

Sky-High Living
ON CHICAGO'S MICHIGAN AVENUE

A COMFORTABLE AND CONVENIENT PIED-À-TERRE,
A SPACE THAT WAS WARM AND ELEGANT AND BELIED THE FACT
IT WAS A NEW APARTMENT IN A MODERN BUILDING.

While these homeowners loved their current residence in the Virginia countryside, they missed the excitement and energy of big-city living in their hometown Chicago. So they purchased an apartment in a downtown Michigan Avenue high-rise with sweeping views of the city and Lake Michigan. Barry had designed their country home and understood their needs—a comfortable and convenient pied-à-terre, a space that was warm and elegant and belied the fact it was a new apartment in a modern building.

A FOYER ANTECHAMBER
is delineated with bronze
Watts of Westminster silk
portieres and an upholstered
seating niche. An "Orsini"
Fortuny pillow in bayou
green and gold adds to
the sense of luxury, while a
"Tatiana" smoked Mercury
glass chandelier from Baker
hangs above, *facing.*

THE BALCONY OPENS
off the living room with
sweeping views of
downtown Chicago and
Lake Michigan. Comfortable
furnishings include a
"Montecito" loveseat and
a pair of bronze "Klismos"
chairs, all from Michael
Taylor; Giati "Mohave Dijon"
was chosen as upholstery
for outdoor wear, *right.*

here would, of course, be significant spatial limitations: rooms were small, windows were oddly placed, and ceilings were low. So Barry began with the most important step—careful measuring. Every inch of the apartment was measured from floor to ceiling, including each window (no two were precisely the same), and a detailed space plan was developed so that furnishings would fit perfectly. Even the widths of the door frames, the dimensions of the common hall outside and the freight elevator and loading dock were carefully notated to avoid any unforeseen snafus. The owners had a few requests: a desk and study area in the master bedroom, a formal dining table that could accommodate family holiday dinners, and an open and accessible kitchen.

A warm and welcoming antechamber was created in the front entry for a sense of anticipation and to lead into the remainder of the apartment. Silk portieres were hung on either side of the front door and repeated across a seated niche built into the end of the passage. Lined with Larson "Aurora" grasscloth, button tufted for a rich and luxurious allure, the niche entices visitors inside and is a perfect spot to take off coats and leave packages.

The living room was painted with Farrow & Ball's sunny "Ciara Yellow," and an urbane palette was created of warm golds and cool grays. A plush Tibetan wool carpet from Odegard was chosen to ground the room. As Chicago is known for its architectural heritage, Barry reflected the city's presence with carefully chosen accents of sophisticated Art Deco design, including a pair of streamlined "Follot" chairs from Niermann Weeks. Set in front of the windows, the chairs were covered in acid citrine "Velours Olympia" from Clarence House, and to create an illusion of height above the windows, panels of Sanderson's cream and yellow "Laburnum" were deliberately inset within the window soffits. A chaise was placed in front of the fireplace, a comfortable spot to watch the fire on cold Chicago nights, while a custom long and low sofa was situated across the room. Built in two sections to allow it to fit into the freight elevator, the sofa was upholstered in Clarence House's woven, maize-colored "Broadlands" to complement the yellow walls. Inspired by Chicago's famed Botanical Gardens, Barry hung a pair of grisaille Zuber panels above either end of the sofa, purposefully tucking them behind it to give an illusion of taller walls and ceilings. Barry's "Dana" ottoman upholstered in Northcroft's honey-toned "Rochelle" cotton velvet was placed in front of the sofa, and matching Murano glass "Gigante" floor lamps from Donghia were placed on either end, bringing the towering urban landscape indoors.

LOOKING INTO the living room from the entry hall, the room appears taller with the Sanderson "Laburnum" draperies set into the window soffits. A carved marble table from Odegard complements a round "Dana" ottoman in the center of the room. A thick Tibetan wool carpet anchors the room, *above*.

GOLDEN TONES— citrine, maize, bronze and ochre—make the living room warm and inviting even on the chilliest Chicago days. The yellow walls highlight a gilt bronze and lacquer table from Dennis & Leen. Streamlined "Follot" chairs from Niermann Weeks rest in front of the window, *facing*.

"LABURNUM" drapery panels from Sanderson were purposefully hung within the soffit outlines to make the ceiling seem taller; the Zuber panel extends to the floor for a similar effect. A curved seagrass rug, Barry's "Albemarle" dining chairs and a tulip-base dining table from New Classics help diminish the room's angularity, *left*.

KITCHEN DESIGNER Mick De Giulio helped create a warm yet streamlined kitchen. Walls and ceiling are covered in golden textured raffia to absorb sound, and a center island serves for both food prep and impromptu meals, *facing*.

The dining room was a challenge, with corner windows, low structural soffits and odd angles. To reinforce an illusion of space and continuity with the living room, Barry again hung "Laburnum" curtains within the window frame, their design of gently trailing wisteria complemented by large, hand-painted Zuber panels hung on the far wall. Titled "Les Lointains," it is an 1825 classic design of urns in the Italian countryside. Curves were introduced to soften the room's angles with a custom burled walnut dining table, Barry's "Albemarle" chairs covered, again, in Watts of Westminster's honey-colored "Charmian" silk, and a round seagrass rug underneath.

Working with kitchen designer Mick De Giulio, a warm and welcoming modern kitchen was created. The walls and ceiling were covered with straw-colored raffia to

absorb sound. Streamlined golden birch cabinets accented with granite counters and backsplashes, brushed steel appliances and a figured stone floor were combined to give the kitchen an urbane and sophisticated appeal. A trio of "Venise" lights from Objets Insolite with crisp card shades were suspended over the center island that, set with a pair of oak counter chairs, is just right for the morning paper and a quick cup of coffee. An L-shaped banquette was built at the end of the room, making a cozy corner for a simple meal while gazing out over the city. Upholstered in a leafy cornflower and yellow print, the banquette wraps around a round concrete table from Concrete Jungle and is lit by a pendant light overhead.

"TUVALU," a nubby duck egg blue silk blend from Robert Allen covers the walls and hangs as draperies in the family room. Roman shades in teal and ivory "Charleston Stripe" from Peter Fasano are a colorful vertical accent. A Chinese-inspired "Macau" coffee table from Dennis & Leen centers the room, *facing*.

WINDOW-LIKE GRIDS of panels of eighteenth-century hand-colored engravings hang above a rainforest green sleeper sectional from Swaim. The "Grand Diego" iron floor lamp is from Objets Insolite, *right*.

CONCENTRIC CIRCLES of Vervain "Crop Circles" on a Julia Gray "Deco" chair are repeated in the Deco-inspired swirls of the "Cloud" Oushak-style rug, *below*.

The family room opens off the kitchen, and for a pleasing contrast, the walls were upholstered in duck egg blue, the fabric continued as draperies on the windows. The ceiling was painted with Farrow & Ball "Blue Green" for a watery accent, and aqua tones were continued underneath in the hand-spun Himalayan wool Oushak-style rug from Odegard. A pair of Julia Gray "Deco" club chairs covered in a cocoa brown and soft blue circle print provides comfortable seating along with a sleeper sofa that doubles as an extra bed for overnight guests.

A BED FROM IRONIES is given feminine appeal with blush pink and chocolate bed hangings and coverlet, *facing*.

SOFT, FEMININE colors and furnishings were chosen for the guest bedroom—a camellia-colored "Helios-Biaggo" carpet from Floor Gallery; cocoa, coral and ivory linen "Serengeti" drapery from Peter Fasano; with cream-colored Conrad shades behind. Barry's "Simone" ivory leather chest-on-stand hides the television, *left*.

A CUSTOM "PARIS" table by David Iatesta finished in a delicate faux parchment wash rests by the side of the bed, *below*.

A guest bedroom at the end of the central hallway was purposefully kept bright and feminine in pretty tones of pinks and chocolate for the owners' daughters, who are frequent visitors. As the room was small, Barry limited the number of patterns and colors to keep it simple. Walls were upholstered in Hines' creamy "Catalina" linen, while the ceiling was highlighted with Farrow & Ball "Fowler Pink" for a rosy glow. Zippy blush and chocolate fabric was used for both the draperies and Barry's skirted "Norma" lounge chair at the foot of the bed. A whitewashed iron bed was dressed with complementary fabrics. Dark chocolate and blush bed curtains, and the coverlet as well, were outlined with Espresso-colored "Cambridge" braid trim from Samuel & Sons.

STROHEIM & ROMANN
"Togo" glazed linen is used for both the headboard and the inner bed curtains. An "Italian Round Side Table" by Julia Gray features a classic Greek key carved border, *below*.

The master bedroom was designed as a serene and inviting private escape for the clients and yet is reflective of the city outside. The room was quieted with walls upholstered in mist-colored "Waxed Linen" from Peter Fasano, and an engaging pistachio and cream linen was used for the curtains as well as the bed coverlet and outer curtains. The window grid of neighboring high-rises was referenced with a group of eighteenth-century Italian engravings by Claude Lorraine, densely hung on the wall in a similar grid-like arrangement. Barry's "Barrymore" chair and a settee covered in taupe "Cavalieri" from Quadrille provide a comfortable area for reading at the foot

of the tester bed, while a richly grained burled walnut desk was nestled in front of the window as a work space for the owner. The adjoining master bath was centered on a large soaking tub from Kohler, floated in front of the large window. Colors and patterns were continued from the bedroom, including "Angelico" linen draperies and Conrad shades.

With careful measuring and planning, and subtle choices of colors and designs reflective of the urban setting, Barry transformed the stark high-rise apartment into an elegant city home, one that welcomes the owners back whenever they come to town.

A PLASMA television screen is hidden inside a Hickory Chair cabinet by Mariette Himes Gomez, *above*.

A BEAUTIFULLY carved and gilded "Kempner" canopy bed by Michael Taylor centers the master bedroom. Pistachio and cream "Angelico" linen is used for window draperies, bed curtains and the coverlet as well, *facing*.

Barry's **Tips**

Use sumptuous fabrics to bring quiet elegance into the foyer.

Reflect the elements of a city view inside: a grid of artwork on the wall; iron, glass and concrete finishes.

Try deconstructed colors and finishes in an urban environment—warm grays, edgy yellows.

Hang art lower to make a wall seem taller.

Upholster kitchen walls and ceilings with fabrics and textures to absorb street noise and make the room more inviting.

Show House
INSPIRATIONS

Show houses are meant to inspire. They are stages where designers can showcase their latest concepts and provide exciting new ideas for their audiences. A show house is much like a laboratory, a place to experiment and be creative in ways that are often not possible elsewhere. To illustrate Barry's thoughts and sources of inspiration, we will look at five of his favorite show houses, ranging from a newly constructed Andalusian-style home perched above the Pacific Ocean in Montecito, California, to a nineteenth-century New York townhouse near Central Park, showing how a home's past can be reinterpreted to create a stylish and vibrant interior for modern living. And that, after all, is what good design inspiration is all about.

Design House
CHEVY CHASE

CHEVY CHASE, MARYLAND

THIS ROOM in a traditional historic Georgian home was once the ballroom. Since the days of ballrooms are past, Barry decided to bring it forward as a comfortable winter garden conservatory and library—a room that reflects the views outdoors and also functions as an inviting retreat to escape with a good book on a winter afternoon. The patina of the garden is echoed inside with complementary materials and finishes: earthenware and terra-cotta, weathered wooden lattices and crusty zinc finishes. A sunny palette of golds, yellows and ochres mixes with earthy stones and grays (including Farrow & Ball's drab "London Stone" on the walls) to emphasize an organic nature. Barry used his collection of fabrics for Vervain along with furnishings he designed for Tomlinson, *left*.

THE GARDEN is brought inside with fluted columns inspired by those on the adjacent terrace.

Made into rotating bookcases for gardening books, the columns' neoclassical design references classic Italian landscaping.

Capital Design House
FOR *SOUTHERN ACCENTS*

MCLEAN, VIRGINIA

A CLASSICAL MUSIC ROOM
with a zesty twist was the
inspiration for this interior in a
Southern Accents magazine show
house. Barry chose bright and
nontraditional color combinations
to add a sense of drama to the
more formal furnishings, with
Farrow & Ball "Ciara Yellow" on
the walls and "Orangerie" on
the ceiling. Playful accents of
magenta and brown punctuate
the carpet. The seriousness of the
classic Empire settee contrasts
with a vintage, lyre-shaped tole
shop sign. Flouncy skirted side
chairs by Mariette Himes Gomez
dance around the room.

"Weekend Living in Montecito" Show House
FOR *TRADITIONAL HOME*

MONTECITO, CALIFORNIA

FAR EASTERN influences play an important role in West Coast design, as Barry reflects with accents such as a delicately carved Burmese chair and a Chinese lamp. The burnt sienna hues of the limestone floor inspired the overall palette of the art and soft furnishings, *above*.

THIS SHOW HOME'S southern Californian setting was Barry's inspiration for its design. He reinterpreted Hollywood glamour with regional references to Spanish architecture. Natural materials, including stone walls and floors, are accented with inlaid panels of limed oak on the ceilings, designed with Harrison & Associates Architects. Heavy woven velvet panels from Quadrille flank the French doors, and four richly upholstered chairs in the center of the room divide the large space into more intimate seating arrangements, *facing*.

FOG THAT ROLLS IN off the Pacific Ocean each morning was the inspiration for the serene master bedroom. Farrow & Ball "Borrowed Light" applied to Venetian plaster walls gives the room a shimmery, misty glow. Silks and satins in pewter silver add to the feel of old Hollywood silent screen glamour, *left*.

THE LIBRARY evokes the lushness of a vintage movie theater, with walls covered not in velvet but acoustic cork block printed with overscale cartouches in dark brown and coffee. Forest green velvet draperies also absorb sound and add to the movie theater atmosphere, while a thick wool carpet from Megerian

in another bold, organic design enhances the play of patterns, *above*.

JEAN HARLOW would have been at home lounging on this bed with its tailored Donghia silk pillows and coverlet. A silver creamer repurposed as a flower vase is an elegant accent, *below*.

A "BOHEMIAN PRINCESS" was the inspiration for the daughter's room, whose walls were upholstered in printed linen from Raoul Textiles in frothy pinks, rosy apricots, fuchsia and purples. Not afraid to mix inexpensive accents in a child's room, Barry selected the overhead lamp from Urban Outfitters for less than $14. The pair of silver Bombay chests is a lighter alternative to one large and bulky dresser, *above*.

A YOUNG GIRL'S love of color is seen here on her bed. A Cameroon headdress made of vermilion-dyed hen feathers hangs above pillows made from a mélange of exotic embroidered textiles in robust hues of fuchsia and hot pink, *above*.

THE GUESTHOUSE, inspired by Japanese shogun architecture, is kept open and elemental. A freestanding partial wall across the center acts as a screen between the living and sleeping areas. Bands of teak wood shingles on the ceiling overlapping like fish scales add to the Oriental effect, *right*.

"Built for Women" Show House
ROOM FOR DIANE SAWYER

MANHATTAN, NEW YORK

A SHOW HOUSE on New York's Madison Avenue featuring ten inspirational women was created as a charity event in the fight against breast cancer. Diane Sawyer asked Barry to design her room. She wanted a cocoon, a very personal space where she could curl up and escape the pressures of the busy city around her. So Barry took her at her word, deftly dissecting an actual cocoon from his garden, then magnifying the patterns of its delicately woven walls and transforming them into a hand-painted, textured finish enveloping the room. Accents celebrating Diane's Kentucky roots include a gilded bronze horse head over the mantel and a large eighteenth-century equestrian-themed screen that provides perspective in the otherwise viewless room. Furnishings in her favorite colors of creams, cocoas and subtle roses make the room a very personal retreat.

The Homestead Preserve Show House
FOR *SOUTHERN ACCENTS*

WARM SPRINGS, VIRGINIA

THE LIVING ROOM is framed by views of the Shenandoah Mountains, so Barry pulled the colors of the countryside indoors with an antique carpet from Moattar in willow green, paprika, burnished gold and bronze. The walls and inset ceiling panels are covered with Laurie Weitzner's gilded rice paper for a soft and inviting glow. Note the plush mattress-like edge of Barry's "Drake" sofa for Tomlinson—an extra touch of comfort and luxury, *left*.

IN THE FAMILY room, comfortable furnishings orbit around the chandelier, *above right*.

A HAND-HAMMERED silver-over-wood cabinet from Odegard centers the master bedroom antechamber, *right*.

A HAMMERED-COPPER bedside table from Odegard references the mineral baths down the hill, as does the alabaster lamp (alabaster being an element frequently brought to the surface by the springs). A bed coverlet and pillow shams in a Peter Fasano hand-painted linen in moss, gold and stone are an appropriately woodsy complement, *above left*.

BARRY GATHERED specimens of local ferns and plants from the countryside and had them painted onto the walls of the master bath to continue the feeling of camping in the forest. A shimmering hammered-silver and teakwood chair from Odegard and a gunmetal tub from Waterworks reinforce the room's elemental organic appeal, *below left*.

INSPIRED BY THE daydream of a glamorous tent pitched in the woods, Barry added a bowed ceiling to the master bedroom and brought the forest inside with dreamy murals of saplings painted on the walls. The bed canopy is hung with hand-blocked silk sheers from John Robshaw in a delicate pattern of leaves to further emphasize the al fresco feeling. Barry's "Germaine" sofa, upholstered with a stone-colored textured linen from Kathryn Ireland, rests at the foot of the bed, *right*.

Charityworks Greenhouse Show House

MCLEAN, VIRGINIA

THE DINING AREA is screened from the kitchen with a wall of metal mesh that allows guests to interact with the hostess while food is prepared. S. Harris fabric on the banquette is made from recycled plastic water bottles, and floor lamps are made of recycled metal and wood. A sustainable balsa wood chandelier hangs overhead. Note the shelves are filled with home-canned, pesticide-free produce from Barry's farm.

LIGHT IS REFLECTED into the room with a salvaged factory window whose glass has been replaced with recycled mirrors. An oversized cheese crate is reborn as a table, *right*.

BARRY'S MISSION for this showhouse was to create a carbon neutral structure with the best of environmentally friendly, sustainable design. Working with eco-savvy architect Mark Turner, he partitioned the main room into a triptych of living spaces for easy casual living. A soft gray Karistan rug made from recycled carpets defines the living area. Carefully selected furnishings include Barry's "Michael" sofa covered in an eco-friendly cotton velvet from Schumacher and a pair of "Barrymore" chairs upholstered in a Lucy Rose sustainable printed linen. Farrow & Ball "Yellow Ground" on the walls and "Elephant's Breath" on the ceiling give the room a sunny warmth, *above*.

RIVETED SHEETS of recycled metal cover the mantelpiece. The hearth is made from rubble recast into stone; a sculptural wooden ring crafted from recycled wood rests on top, *facing*.

EXPOSURE MARY ELLEN MARK

ICONS OF THE 20TH CENTURY
200 MEN AND WOMEN WHO HAVE MADE A DIFFERENCE

Resources

ANTIQUES

1st Dibs
www.1stdibs.com-good

Amy Perlin
www.amyperlinantiques.com

Antiques on 5
www.antiqueson5.com

Antiques on Old Plank Road
www.oldplank.com

Ceylon et Cie
www.ceylonetcie.com

Côté Jardin Antiques
www.cotejardinantiques.com

David Bell
Tel: 202-965-2355

David Duncan Antiques
www.davidduncanantiques.com

DHS Designs
www.dhsdesigns.com

E.J. Grant
www.grantantiques.com

Stephane Oliver
www.stephaneolivier.fr

Florian Papp, Inc.
www.florianpapp.com

Gore-Dean
www.goredean.com

H.M. Luther, Inc.
www.hmluther.com

Hastenings
www.hasteningantiques.com

J.F. Chen
www.jfchen.com

John Gregory Studio
www.johngregorystudio.com

John Rosselli & Associates, Ltd.
www.johnroselliantiques.com

Kenny Ball Antiques
www.kennyballantiques.com

Kentshire Galleries
www.kentshire.com

Lee Stanton Antiques
www.leestanton.com

Maison Gerard, Ltd.
www.maisongerard.com

Marvin Alexander, Inc.
www.marvinalexanderinc.com

Miller and Arney
www.millerarney.com

Randall Tysinger
www.randalltysinger.com

Suzanne Golden Antiques
www.suzannegoldenantiques.com

ARTISANS

Agora Interiors
Tel: 703-823-7800

Architectural Ceramics
www.architecturalceramics.net

Avery Fine Art
www.averyart.com

Concrete Jungle
www.concretejungleonline.com

Halgren O'Brien
Tel: 540-341-7527

Kelly Metalworks
Tel: 301-854-4848

Konst Construction
www.konstlifestyle.com

Lobkovich, Inc.
www.lobkovich.com

Mitchell Yanosky
www.mitchellyanosky.com

Natural Curiosities
www.naturalcuriosities.com

Old Town Woodworking
www.oldtownwoodworking.com

Portfolio Kitchens
www.portfoliokitchens.com

Renaissance Tile
www.renaissancetileandbath.com

Warnock Studios
www.warnockstudios.com

Waterworks
www.waterworks.com

CARPETS

AMS Imports, Inc.
www.amsimports.com

Elizabeth Eakins
www.elizabetheakins.com

Floor Gallery
www.thefloorgallery.com

Kyle Bunting
www.kylebunting.com

Megerian
www.megerianrugs.com

Odegard
www.odegardinc.com

Stark
www.starkcarpet.com

Timothy Paul
www.timothypaulcarpets.com

TEXTILES

Bennison
www.bennisonfabrics.com

Bergamo
www.bergamofabrics.com

Brunschwig and Fils
www.brunschwig.com

Camilla David Textiles
www.camilladavidtextiles.com

Chelsea Editions
www.chelseaeditions.com

China Seas
www.quadrillefabrics.com

Clarence House
www.clarencehouse.com

Conrad
www.conradshades.com

Cowtan and Tout
www.cowtan.com

Donghia
www.donghia.com

Duralee
www.duralee.com

Elitis
www.elitis.fr

Fortuny
www.fortuny.com

Giati Designs, Inc.
www.giati.com

Gisbert-Rentmeister
Tel: 202-646-1774

Glant Textiles
www.glant.com

Gracie Studio
www.graciestudio.com

Henry Calvin
www.henrycalvin.com

Highland Court
www.highlandcourtfabrics.com

Hodsoll McKenzie
Tel: 800-996-9607

Holland & Sherry
www.hollandandsherry.com

Home Couture Textile/Quadrille
www.quadrillefabrics.com

J. Robert Scott
www.jrobertscott.com

Jasper Fabrics
www.jasperfabrics.com

John Robshaw Textiles
www.johnrobshaw.com

Kathryn Ireland
www.kathrynireland.com

Kravet
www.kravet.com

Larsen
www.cowtan.com

Lee Jofa
www.leejofa.com

Lucy Rose Design
www.lucyrosedesign.com

Lulu DK
www.luludk.com

Manuel Canovas
www.manuelcanovas.com

Martyn Lawrence-Bullard Designs
www.martynlawrencebullard.com

Morris and Co.
www.william-morris.co.uk

Myung Jin
www.myungjinfabric.com

Northcroft Fabrics
www.northcroftfabrics.co.uk

Old World Weavers
www.fonthill-ltd.com

Osborne and Little
www.osborneandlittle.com

Peter Fasano
www.peterfasano.com

Phillip Jeffries, Ltd.
www.phillipjeffries.com

Pierre Frey
www.pierrefrey.com

Pintura Studio
www.pinturastudio.com

Pollack
www.pollackassociates.com

Quadrille
www.quadrillefabrics.com

Raoul Textiles
www.raoultextiles.com

Robert Kime
www.robertkime.com

Rogers and Goffigon
Tel: 203-532-8068

S. Harris
www.sharris.com

Sabrina Fay Braxton
www.sabinafaybraxton.com

Sanderson
www.sanderson-uk.com

Scalamandré
www.Scalamandré.com

Schumacher and Co.
www.fschumacher.com

Sea Cloth
www.seacloth.com

Sister Parish
www.sisterparishdesign.com

Stroheim & Romann
www.stroheim.com

Tyler Graphics
www.tylergraphic.com

Twill
www.twilltextiles.com

Valtekz
www.valtekz.com

Vervain
www.vervain.com

Watts of Westminster
www.wattsofwestminster.com

Zimmer and Rhode
www.zimmer-rohde.com

Zoffany
www.zoffany.com

Zuber Cie
www.zuber.fr

FURNITURE LINES

Amy Howard
www.amyhowardcollection.com

Avrett
www.avrett.com

Barry Dixon Collection
www.barrydixon.com

Bauserman & Co.
www.bausman.net

Beeline Home
www.bunnywilliams.com/beeline

Bolier & Co.
www.bolierco.com

Cameron Collection
www.cameroncollection.com

Carole Gratale
www.carolegratale.com

Charles Pollock
www.charlespollockrepro.com

Christian Liaigre
www.christian-liaigre.fr

Coup d'Etat
www.coupdetat.1stdibs.com

David Iatesta
www.davidiatesta.com

Dennis and Leen
www.dennisandleen.com

Dessin Fournir
www.dessinfournir.com

Formations
www.formationsusa.com

Fourhands
www.fourhands.com

Gregorius-Pineo
www.gregoriuspineo.com

George Smith
www.georgesmith.com

Giati
www.giati.com

Grange Furniture, Inc.
www.grange.fr

Helene Aumont
www.heleneaumont.com

Hickory Chair
www.hickorychair.com

Ironies
www.ironies.com

Ironware International
www.ironwareinternational.com

Janus et Cie
www.janusetcie.com

Jasper Furniture
www.jasperfabrics.com

Jean de Merry
www.jeandemerry.com

Jiun Ho Collection
www.jiunho.com

Julia Gray
www.juliagraymindwire.com

Julian Chichester
www.julianchichester.com

Kneedler-Fauchere
Tel: 310-855-1313

Edward Ferrell/Lewis Mittman
www.ef-lm.com

Madeline Stuart
www.madelinestuart.com

McGuire
www.mcguirefurniture.com

Michael Taylor
www.michaeltaylordesigns.com

Mike Reid Weeks
Tel: 843-851-6968

Mitchell-Yanosky
www.mitchellyanosky.com

New Classics
www.newclassics.biz

Niermann Weeks
www.niermannweeks.com

O. Henry House
www.ohenryhouseltd.com

Objet Insolite
www.objetinsolite.com

Ochre
www.ochre.net

Oly
www.olystudio.com

Panache Designs
www.panachedesigns.com

Patina
www.patinainc.com

Pierce Martin
www.piercemartin.com

R. Jones
www.rjones.com

Rose Tarlow - Melrose House
www.rosetarlow.com

Ruth Livingston Studio
www.ruthlivingston.com

W. & J. Sloane
www.wandjsloane.com

Stewart Furniture
www.stewartfurniture.com

Stone Yard, Inc.
www.stoneyardinc.com

Sutherland
www.sutherlandteak.com

Tisserant Art & Style
www.tisserant.fr

Tomlinson/Erwin-Lambeth
www.tomlinsonerwinlambeth.com

Baker
www.bakerfurniture.com

William Switzer
www.williamswitzercollection.com

Zentique
www.zentique.com

SHOWROOMS

Ailanthus Ltd
www.ailanthusltd.com

Ainsworth Noah
www.ainsworth-noah.com

Anthropologie
www.anthropologie.com

Dean Warren Assoc.
www.deanwarren.com

Designer's Market
www.designers-market.com

Donghia
www.donghia.com

Harsey & Harsey
www.harseyandharsey.com

Hinc
www.hincshowroom.com

Hines and Co.
www.hinesyang.com

Holly Hunt
www.hollyhunt.com

J. Lambeth
www.jlambeth.com

John Brooks, Inc
www.johnbrooksinc.com

John Rosselli
www.johnrosselliantiques.com

KDR Designer Showrooms
www.kdrshowrooms.com

Michael Cleary
Tel: 202-488-9787

Patricia Group
www.patriciagroup.com

R. Hughes
www.r-hughes.com

Smith Grubbs
www.smithgrubbs.com

The Martin Group
www.martingroupinc.com

Treillage
www.bunnywilliams.com/treillage

Thanks to the staff at Barry Dixon, Inc., who help make all of these beautiful interiors possible:

Gladys Marilu Barrera
Rachel Brown
Dabney Doswell
Cathy Foster
Allison Kijak
Teri Kreitzer
Catherine LeBlanc
Laurel Mitchell
Nicole Rossetti
Kristine Weir
Michael Schmidt
Gladys Marilu Barrera

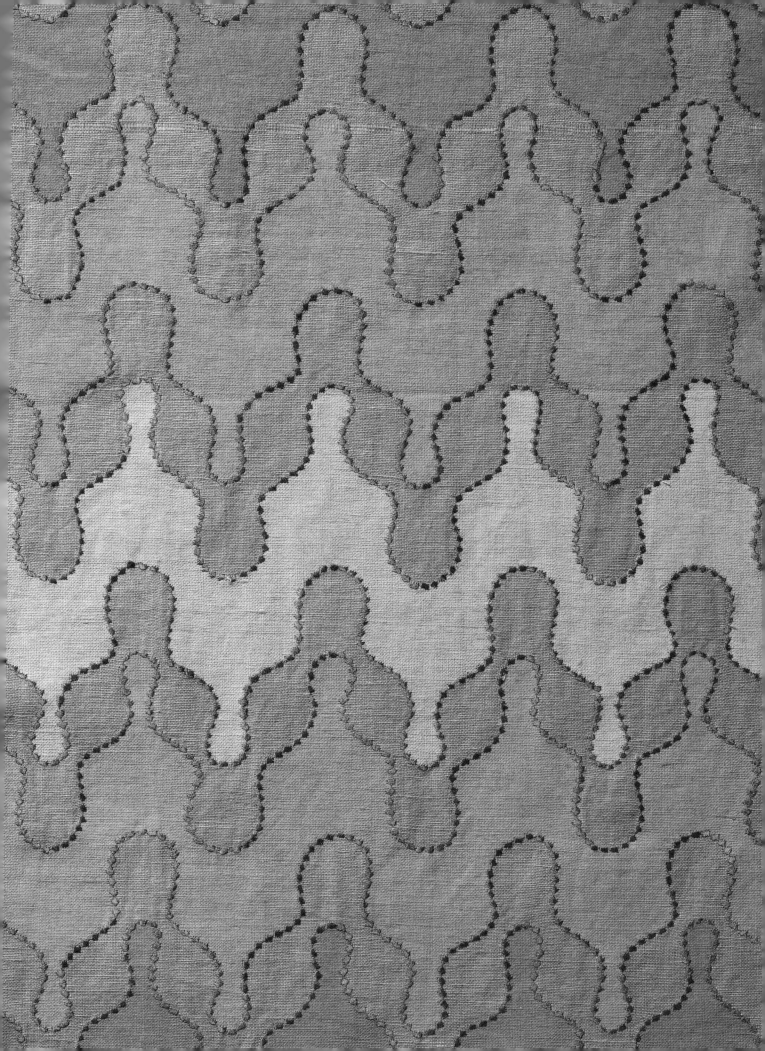

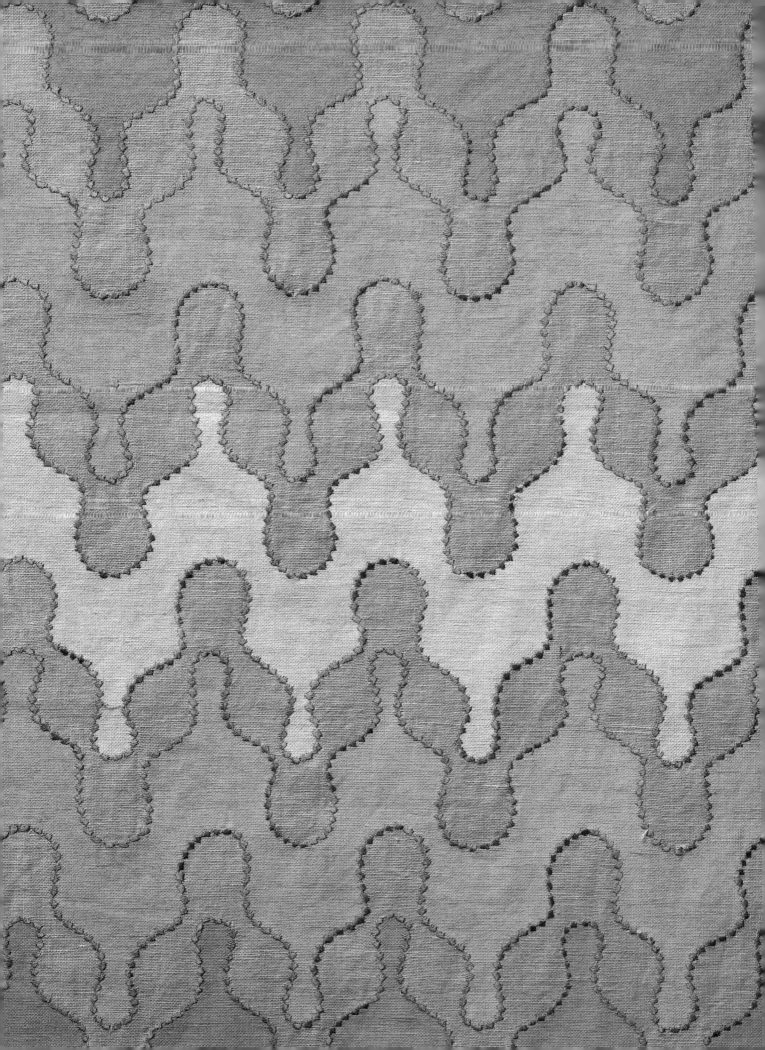